Jump Rope Training
Second Edition

Buddy Lee

Human Kinetics

Library of Congress Cataloging-in-Publication Data

Lee, Buddy, 1958-
  Jump rope training / Buddy Lee. -- 2nd ed.
    p. cm.
  ISBN-13: 978-0-7360-8159-7 (soft cover)
  ISBN-10: 0-7360-8159-3 (soft cover)
  1. Rope skipping. 2. Physical fitness. I. Title.
  GV498.L44 2010
  796.2--dc22

                          2010006722

ISBN-10: 0-7360-8159-3 (print)
ISBN-13: 978-0-7360-8159-7 (print)

Copyright © 2010 by Jump-Aerobics, Inc.
          © 2003 by Anthony N. Lee

This publication is written and published to provide accurate and authoritative information relevant to the subject matter presented. It is published and sold with the understanding that the author and publisher are not engaged in rendering legal, medical, or other professional services by reason of their authorship or publication of this work. If medical or other expert assistance is required, the services of a competent professional person should be sought.

The Web addresses cited in this text were current as of March 2010, unless otherwise noted.

Acquisitions Editor: Laurel Plotzke Garcia; **Developmental Editor:** Kevin Matz; **Assistant Editor:** Elizabeth Evans; **Copyeditor:** Tom Tiller; **Permission Manager:** Martha Gullo; **Graphic Designer and Graphic Artist:** Julie L. Denzer; **Cover Designer:** Keith Blomberg; **Photographer (cover):** Tom Roberts; **Photographer (interior):** Tom Roberts, unless otherwise noted; **Photo Asset Manager:** Laura Fitch; **Visual Production Assistant:** Joyce Brumfield; **Photo Production Manager:** Jason Allen; **Art Manager:** Kelly Hendren; **Associate Art Manager:** Alan L. Wilborn; **Illustrator:** Mic Greenberg; **Printer:** United Graphics

Human Kinetics books are available at special discounts for bulk purchase. Special editions or book excerpts can also be created to specification. For details, contact the Special Sales Manager at Human Kinetics.

Printed in the United States of America   10 9 8 7 6 5 4 3 2

The paper in this book is certified under a sustainable forestry program.

Human Kinetics
Web site: www.HumanKinetics.com

United States: Human Kinetics
P.O. Box 5076
Champaign, IL 61825-5076
800-747-4457
e-mail: humank@hkusa.com

Canada: Human Kinetics
475 Devonshire Road Unit 100
Windsor, ON N8Y 2L5
800-465-7301 (in Canada only)
e-mail: info@hkcanada.com

Europe: Human Kinetics
107 Bradford Road
Stanningley
Leeds LS28 6AT, United Kingdom
+44 (0) 113 255 5665
e-mail: hk@hkeurope.com

Australia: Human Kinetics
57A Price Avenue
Lower Mitcham, South Australia 5062
08 8372 0999
e-mail: info@hkaustralia.com

New Zealand: Human Kinetics
P.O. Box 80
Torrens Park, South Australia 5062
0800 222 062
e-mail: info@hknewzealand.com

E4755

Acknowledgments

A special dedication goes out to my mom, Mittie Lee, who raised six children by herself. She is a true champion who taught me life skills and spirituality and provided a good home environment for beginning my life's journey.

To Herbert Rainey Jr., a master martial artist, mentor, next-door neighbor, and friend who introduced me to the jump rope when I was a teenager. His lesson inspired me to become a champion wrestler and laid the foundation to my jump rope training system today.

To Anna Sandwall, vice president of Jump Rope Technology Inc. and my great friend who has shared my dream since 1994. In both good times and bad, she has remained committed, enthusiastic, and focused on developing my vision into a complete concept of patented products, programs, and services. As a team, we have inspired millions around the world to jump into fitness.

It takes a community of family, friends, and educators to help shape and develop a child into an Olympian. A special thanks goes out to my brothers and sisters: Jessie, Joe, Cynthia, Brenda, and Jonathan. And thanks to my children: Letisha and Noah. And thanks to my close friends: Craig Bethke, Hamid Negati, Arnold Tobin, and Malcolm Pugh.

To Laurel Plotzke Garcia for her confidence, support, and enthusiasm in proposing this second edition and for assigning my developmental editor, Kevin Matz, and his incredible team who kept me on track and advised me in order to maintain good content throughout the book. To Dr. Ray Tademy for his lifelong support and advanced insight and understanding of how to communicate my jump rope training system to the world. To World Jump Rope Champion, Elvis Malcolm, and to Dr. Emily Splichal and Gray Cook, author of *Body in Balance*, for their contributions.

To the many ambassadors of my jump rope training system who have helped me to inspire millions of people around the world to jump the correct way. Finally to all coaches, athletes, and business partners who stood by me over the years during both the good times and the tough times to help me become the man I am today.

Rope to success!

Contents

Preface

Ifirst became curious about rope jumping after watching my next-door neighbor, Herbert Rainey, a fourth-degree black belt in karate, jump rope every day as part of his martial arts training. He knew my goal of becoming the best wrestler in Virginia and told me that rope jumping would not only increase my fitness but also make me quicker. *Quicker?* I was already quick, and the idea of becoming even quicker intrigued me.

One day, I begged him to teach me how to jump rope. He stopped his workout and showed me the two basic jump rope techniques. They seemed simple at the time, but I now realize that he introduced me to the foundation of any jump rope training program. After Herbert taught me those basic movements, I wanted to master them as quickly as I could so that I could move on to other techniques. My first jump rope session lasted into the night. By the time I stopped, I had spent 5 hours practicing the basic bounce and the alternate-foot step

I incorporated rope jumping into my wrestling training program as a sophomore at Highland Springs High School, which was known for its state championship teams in basketball and football. Rudy Ward was my wrestling coach, teacher, father figure, and true friend. He played an important role in my life and made all the difference in helping me become the school's first state wrestling champion; later, he would even fly to Barcelona to watch me wrestle in the 1992 Olympic Games. After I graduated from high school, other Springer wrestlers followed in my footsteps, and Highland Springs High School soon became recognized as a wrestling powerhouse in Virginia.

I vividly recall the basics of my strength and conditioning program: doing push-ups (I used a deck of cards as a guide to decide the number of push-ups I would do in one set. I would shuffle the deck of cards and lay them on the floor face down. I would pull a card from the deck and the number of push-ups I performed was determined by the number of the card I turned over, where a face card represented 10 reps, an ace card eleven reps, and all others its true value. By the beginning of my second year in high school the number of push-ups I could do in a workout would include the entire deck, which dramatically increased my upper body strength. From there I worked up to a total 1,000 push-ups in 10 sets of 100 reps), doing sit-ups (up to 600 in 6 sets of 100 reps), running very fast around the schoolyard telephone poles, and jumping rope. In fact, rope jumping helped me improve in every aspect of my wrestling ability. It gave me the winning edge!

During my first four years as a US Marine, I became more successful in my wrestling career and also gained international popularity from jump rope demonstrations. The jump rope demos made a positive impact on people of all ages and got them excited to learn more about the ropes. I liked the impression the ropes left on people after a performance and became more determined to achieve my Olympic goal in wrestling in order to make a difference in the world with the jump ropes. My mission in becoming a U.S. Olympian wrestler was ultimately to educate and motivate people in all sports to integrate rope jumping into their training in order to develop a competitive advantage for superior sports performance. Still, the way it has all happened amazes me. I would eventually become jump rope conditioning consultant to U.S. Olympic teams and founder of both Jump Rope Technology, Inc., and the Jump Rope Institute. But I still remember back in 1986 when the United States Olympic Committee (USOC) published its first article about my jump rope training system and how it affected my wrestling. In particular, I remember the article's last sentence, which stated my dream of developing my own jump rope and making jump rope my way of life. I had no idea at that time that training for 10 hours a day for a decade—and making jump rope a key to my own training—would catch the interest of many other sports and fitness programs around the world. My life, and my world, have evolved around getting people to learn the right way to jump rope as a way of life.

The turning point in my jump rope crusade came at the United States Olympic Training Center in Colorado Springs during the 1996 Olympic team trials. During this time the USOC selected Bonnie Blair, a five time Olympic Gold Medalist in Speed Skating, and myself to speak before President Bill Clinton, Vice President Al Gore, and thousands of children at a Champions in Life Program. The Champions in Life Program was held in Washington, D.C. at Eastern High School. It is a community outreach program developed by the USOC where Olympians reach out to inner-city kids to live their dreams and promote the Olympic movement The next day, when I returned to the training center in Colorado Springs, I was greeted with the honor of becoming the official U.S. Olympic conditioning coach. The U.S. women's basketball team asked me to cross-train their Olympic gold medal team in rope jumping in order to help them gain an edge in foot speed and quick jumping. These athletes—including Lisa Leslie, Sheryl Swoopes, Rebecca Lobo, and Teresa Edwards—caught on after a few training sessions and began to take the ropes with them everywhere they went. Rope jumping became a key to their training on the road to Olympic gold. The practice turned out to be contagious, and the Ukrainian and Korean Women's Olympic basketball teams asked me to train their athletes with the same high-intensity programs. They all learned the ropes and were very impressive in jumping ability. In that same week, Kristy Krall, the director of education for U.S. Figure Skating, asked me to work with the skaters. In the belief that rope jumping should be the foundation of all skaters' training programs, she had me work with coaches and skaters for all of the senior and junior national teams. Since then, jump rope has become a key warm-up and dry-land conditioning method in the world of figure skating.

After this experience, I knew I had to learn more about jump rope, and between practice sessions over the years I would go to the library and research this exercise. As a result, I learned how it works, how it provides benefits, and how research studies confirm its incredible rewards. I learned that rope jumping not only provides a great tool for improving athletic performance but also could easily become a means to fitness for people of all ages and abilities around the world. It was through jump rope research and practice that I became a self-made Olympian. I learned how the body works and what it needs in order to perform at its optimal level. I have put this knowledge to use over the years in my own jump rope training, in developing sports specific programs for Olympic teams, and in helping others understand (in as little as 5 minutes) how to maximize the benefits. At this point, my training system has helped athletes in the following sports:

Badminton	Modern pentathlon
Basketball	Shooting
Bobsled	Soccer
Boxing	Swimming
Cross-country skiing	Table tennis
Cycling	Taekwondo
Diving	Track and field
Gymnastics	Volleyball
Judo	Wrestling

This book, then, focuses on an activity that was once viewed simply as something we did as little kids but has evolved into one of most efficient ways to improve cardiovascular health. The book shows you how jump rope training can provide you with benefits that go beyond cardiovascular health. In a time when many people in the United States, and in the world, suffer from physical and mental disease, we need exercises that are functional, inexpensive, and beneficial in multiple ways so that we can attain optimal health. In the process of striving for athletic excellence, I have come to understand how this exercise must be broken down into steps that a beginner can master. As a result, I have created a jump rope training system that redefines jump rope and will change your perspective on what fitness is—and can even change your life.

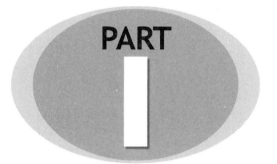

JUMP ROPE
TRAINING PROGRESSION

Introducing the Buddy Lee System

The sports and fitness potential of rope jumping has emerged from the dark gyms used by boxers, martial artists, wrestlers, and other athletes who discovered and eked out its benefits. Today, rope jumping is often featured prominently as part of sports training and fitness programs because it has proven itself as a valuable technique that provides a wide range of benefits and competitive advantages. Sports training benefits include increased speed, power, agility, and explosiveness. Fitness benefits include weight loss, increased cardiovascular and anaerobic conditioning, and improved balance and coordination. Nonetheless, many coaches, fitness trainers, and sports and fitness enthusiasts remain unaware of the full potential of this simple but challenging exercise. And even those coaches and athletes who are already inspired to incorporate rope jumping into their training programs may be unsure just how to tailor these techniques to meet the unique demands of their particular sport.

When done properly, jump rope training can lead to dramatic improvement in sports performance. For example, star baseball players have used rope jumping to improve their grip strength and increase their eye–hand coordination and bat speed. Rope jumping is also used by football players (e.g., Terrell Owens), basketball players (e.g., Kobe Bryant), and soccer players and other athletes who rely upon demanding foot movements (e.g., rapid changes of direction) to improve their balance and proprioception in their ankles and feet in ways that reduce the risk of injury. Bruce Lee, who triggered a martial arts craze in the United States, used rope jumping as a warm-up and as a training strategy to develop timing, balance, quickness, and speed. Today, in the rising sport of mixed martial arts (MMA), jump rope training often serves as a mandatory part of daily training regimens. Boxer Floyd Mayweather Jr. has been seen on Internet videos featuring the high-intensity jump rope routines he used to become a world champion in multiple weight classes, and a number of boxing greats—including Roberto Duran, Sugar Ray Leonard, and Muhammad Ali—were often filmed while they executed rope-jumping routines as part of their prefight training. Rope jumping also plays an important role in the training regimens used by skaters, swimmers, and gymnasts on U.S. Olympic teams.

In this book, I will help *you* tailor a jump rope training routine to match the fitness, energy system needs, and movement demands of *your* sport. My jump rope training system has been tested and proven to work with the world's greatest athletes—including members of U.S. national and Olympic teams and top professional teams (e.g., Chicago White Sox, Cincinnati Bengals, European soccer and rugby teams), as well as members of the U.S. military and participants in the Ultimate Fighting Championship (UFC), CrossFit, TRX Training, and kettlebell training. In addition, as the jump rope conditioning coach for the U.S. Olympic team, I used my system in working with basketball players, wrestlers, swimmers, skaters, gymnasts, and other athletes, including those who played handball and badminton.

My 3-step jump rope training system teaches people of all ages and abilities how to jump with minimal impact and use correct body mechanics, perfect technique, and safe progressions in order to build the necessary endurance to implement and benefit from my high-performance programs. This process requires that you first become proficient at rope jumping, then gradually build your endurance in order to develop basic jump rope capacity. My system is designed to motivate you every step of the way as you work to achieve superior fitness in as little as 5 to 10 minutes a day.

Why Rope Jumping Works

Rope jumping is one of only a few inexpensive, highly portable, and easily learned fitness and sports training exercises that require the precise coordination of several muscle groups. This precise coordination must be attained and maintained during each rope-jumping session. If you perform frequent, sustained rope-jumping sessions, you will quickly improve your capacity for dynamic balance—that is, your ability to maintain equilibrium while executing complex, vigorous, and omnidirectional movements. At the same time, integrating several muscle groups will improve your overall fitness level while also reducing your risk of freak injury (i.e., injury caused by abrupt movement due to an unexpected loss of balance or equilibrium).

Jump Rope Misconceptions and Truths

People around the world hold various misconceptions about rope jumping and generally have little knowledge of its fitness and sports training benefits. Many people think of rope jumping as primarily an activity for young girls; others, in contrast, view it as a risky high-impact exercise that can injure the knees, ankles, and feet. Still others shy away from rope jumping because they see little training or fitness value in it or because they believe that it requires a high level of coordination that will make it difficult to learn. Some people may decide not to jump rope in public spaces, including fitness centers, because they have a low level of coordination and do not want to be perceived as a klutz! However, once they learn about the benefits and use a step-by-step system to learn to jump correctly, these notions can be replaced by a determination to master the basic techniques that will enable them to improve their coordination and balance. Rope jumping should not be feared—it should be embraced as an essential fitness and sports training tool.

If you follow a step-by-step program, you can quickly learn basic rope-jumping skills and increase your proficiency. Rope jumping has been endorsed by the American Heart Association, which advocates it as a way to raise children's physical fitness levels and thus reduce their lifetime risk of heart disease, cardiovascular ailments, and stroke. Rope jumping can also improve brain function because of its influence on the vestibular system in the inner ear, which is responsible for the sense of balance and is linked to specific neuroanatomical systems that govern physical movement. In addition, because rope jumping requires you to coordinate and synchronize a large number of upper- and lower-body muscle groups, it generates significant brain activity in several cortical centers that result in increased kinesthetic awareness and mental alertness. Rope jumping also causes you to expend more calories than do most aerobic activities, thus aiding in weight loss, and it reduces your risk of osteoporosis by increasing your bone density.

A jump rope is portable and requires only a small space to use. But when it is used correctly, it can provide you with significant benefits in weeks or even days, depending on your individual fitness, training level, and personal commitment.

Rope jumping also makes very specific demands upon your mind and body. My jump rope training system builds on these unique mental and physical demands in ways that improve your ability to perform and increase your fitness. These demands include the following:

- Timing the swing of the rope with the act of jumping
- Maintaining a firm grip on the rope handles to resist the centripetal and centrifugal forces of the swinging rope
- Using manual quickness while being light on your feet
- Concentrating to maintain correct jump rope posture and technique

Research Claims

Rope jumping is an extremely effective method for improving cardiovascular health and fitness in a relatively short time. An often-quoted study suggested that 10 minutes of jumping can provide cardiovascular benefits equal to 30 minutes of jogging. These findings were attributed to the multiple systemic demands of rope jumping—especially its emphasis upon multijoint movements that can easily draw upon aerobic and anaerobic energy systems in a 10-minute set. Another study suggested that 5 minutes of daily rope jumping may be enough to quickly raise fitness levels for individuals who rarely exercise.

More recent research studies have shown that rope jumping can increase bone density in ways that reduce injury and the risk of possible degenerative conditions such as osteoporosis. These benefits can be gained by jumping as little as 1 inch (2.5 cm) from the jumping surface (which generates stresses as small as 1.5 to 3 times one's body weight) for as few as three 5-minute sessions per week. One study of youth in Asia found that rope jumping can contribute to increases in running endurance, broad-jumping ability, and upper-body strength; the increases in upper-body strength were attributed to the demands that rope jumping makes upon muscle fibers in the shoulders, back, and chest that are recruited with each turn of the rope.

Other studies report that rope jumping at high-intensity levels (85 percent or higher of an individual's maximum heart rate, or MHR) can produce rapid fitness gains. These intensity levels are equivalent to sprint training sessions which have been found to generate greater training effects than slow-paced plyometric workouts. These findings support my belief that my jump rope sprint training programs can dramatically improve your fitness and performance levels in ways that will give you a significant edge in most sports. I feel strongly about this because although rope jumping may seem to emphasize lower-body muscle groups, it also develops your shoulder, chest, back, wrist, and forearm muscles. In addition, rope jumping primarily recruits fast-twitch muscle fibers, thus helping you create "cuts" (i.e., muscle definition) and increasing your speed and quickness.

Dynamic Balance

Rope jumping increases your dynamic balance because it requires you to make numerous neuromuscular adjustments on each jump. Think about it: During each rope-jumping session, your balance is both lost and achieved hundreds of times. Current research shows that these adjustments are coordinated by your brain, which means that rope jumping can contribute to improved brain function, especially in your motor cortex and cerebellum.

Rope jumping also forces you to repeatedly balance your body weight on the balls of your feet. Doing so reduces stress on your knees while also reinforcing the universal athletic position—a position of readiness that prepares you to react quickly and omnidirectionally. This readiness position is seen when an athlete crouches slightly while balancing his or her body weight on the balls of the feet. One foot can be placed in front of other, depending upon the direction in which the athlete expects to react. For example, a basketball player might assume a defensive position with both palms up and with the arms extended slightly to the side while the body is in a slight crouch and thus prepared for omnidirectional movement (see figure 1.1). A baseball player—particularly an infielder—might assume a similar position in anticipation of reacting to the next hit. A tennis player might also assume this position while waiting for the opponent's serve, and a variation of the universal athletic position can be seen in swimmers waiting on the platform before the start of a race.

Reinforcement of the universal athletic position through rope jumping increases your ability to react quickly and accurately, especially when changing direction. At the same time, as you concentrate on maintaining the rhythm of swinging the rope and

Figure 1.1 The universal athletic position.

jumping over it, you facilitate subtle neuromuscular adjustments with each jump that increase your capacity to make streamlined and efficient movements. Thus the melding of mind and movement is an unspoken secret of how to use jump rope training to improve performance.

Efficient Movements

Efficient movements are especially appreciated by older athletes, who realize that proper technique allows them to conserve energy and employ it strategically. Inefficient movements, in contrast, force the athlete to waste energy and time in trying to compensate; for a vivid example of this kind of waste, watch a tired, unskilled runner's gait—a bobbing head, arms that drag instead of pulling, and a posture that looks like someone about to keel over. With each ragged step, such runners work against themselves. Their efforts to compensate for inefficient movements sap their bodies of energy and reduce their stamina. After a certain point, they might as well walk. This is why many runners are coached to "hold their form." Efficient movements can also create a synergy of quickness, timing, and strength that generates power and explosiveness even as it improves endurance. The energy conserved by moving efficiently reduces distractions caused by pain or discomfort during sports performance.

Rope jumping requires a similar type of mental discipline. Specifically, the jumper maintains moment-to-moment concentration in order to synchronize the precise movements of the several muscle groups that are recruited to execute each jump. This type of concentration, called mindfulness, is a mental discipline used by competitive and professional athletes all over the world. Mindfulness can be described as the ability to maintain concentration on your current activity without being distracted; it is also a technique used by doctors and psychologists to reduce anxiety and fear. It can enable those who practice it to achieve high-level sports and professional performance for extended periods of time. It can also help fitness enthusiasts maximize the benefits of their workout or training techniques even in the midst of stress or other distractions.

Aerobic Capacity—$\dot{V}O_2$max

Moment-to-moment attention to sports performance increases your maximal oxygen uptake ($\dot{V}O_2$max) and unloads more carbon dioxide with each breath. $\dot{V}O_2$max is the maximum amount of oxygen your heart can project into your blood, and thereby into your muscles, during sustained exercise. The more intensely you exercise, the more oxygen you need in order to sustain that intensity. There is, of course, an upper limit to both exercise intensity and your body's capacity to consume oxygen. This limit is your $\dot{V}O_2$max—the point at which your blood is unable to absorb additional oxygen. It is sometimes referred to as your redline zone.

$\dot{V}O_2$max can be reached at a relatively low percentage of your maximum heart rate; for some people, exertion at 91 percent of their maximum heart rate is enough to take them there. The $\dot{V}O_2$max can be experienced in a short, intense burst of sprint jumping for 10 to 30 seconds. Once you increase your fitness level, you will be able to perform high-intensity activity for longer periods of time. This capacity is especially important if your sport demands that you sustain maximum exertion for considerable periods. In such cases, developing a capacity for sustained exertion at your $\dot{V}O_2$max—or anaerobic power—may be the key to maxi-

There is only one right way to jump for better sports performance: You must train with the rope in ways that simulate the movements and energy system demands of your sport. Jump for speed, power, and finesse (precision of movement). For improved fitness and sports performance, my high-intensity or "hyperformance" jump rope training program will enable you to achieve the greatest benefits in the shortest time.

TIP

mizing your endurance potential and your capacity to meet the championship performance demands of your sport.

Thus rope jumping can help you increase your dynamic balance, your moment-to-moment concentration, and your capacity for sustained high-level exertion. As a result, it can help you achieve your desired fitness level and develop the competitive edge required for peak sports performance.

Gaining the Competitive Edge

Victory is often determined by a fraction of a second or a few inches of space. The difference between winning and losing can even be measured in hundredths of a second. At the 2008 Olympics in Beijing, the men's swimming team from the United States won the gold medal in the 4×100 meter freestyle relay by eight-hundredths of a second! Close finishes are, in fact, the norm at world-class competitions, and athletes train for several hours a day for years on end in an effort to cultivate the technique, strategy, or program that will give them that slight edge over their competitors. Edges in time are created by quickness and speed and can be sustained by endurance. For example, I may beat you out of the blocks and be able to run faster, but victory will be determined by whether I *sustain* the edge long enough to win. Blowouts make for dramatic differences between competitors, but they are created by individuals or teams who maintain small advantages in speed, quickness, or efficiency over an extended period of time. If I am one step faster per minute than the rest of the pack, then I can win a marathon by a city block! I can also win if I have the stamina to initiate and sustain a kick at a point in the race where other runners have depleted their energy.

Every athlete aims to establish and maintain an edge in time or space throughout the course of competition. Doing so may take a variety of skills. For example, if you combine quickness and strength, you can create explosiveness and power. If you

© Icon SMI

A jump rope training program can help you develop the agility needed in fast-action basketball play.

TIP

To benefit most from my jump rope training system in the shortest possible time, you should train systematically to develop that championship edge.

combine explosiveness, power, and timing, you can amplify your advantages in quickness and speed. Thus these factors can work together to give you a competitive edge in most sports competitions.

Jump rope training, then, can dramatically improve your sports performance. Specifically, you can use it to fine-tune your neuromuscular adjustments, your precise synchronization of multiple muscle groups, your concentration, and your integration of several elements of the competitive edge that can dramatically enhance your sports performance. My jump rope training system targets the anaerobic energy system and helps you develop speed, quickness, agility, and explosiveness—key factors in gaining and sustaining a competitive edge. Specific programs are included to target each of these factors. My system also helps you develop the following:

- Increased wrist, ankle, and knee strength
- Conditioning of your back, shoulders, and chest
- Increased gripping strength
- Improved posture
- Increased proprioception in your feet and ankles
- Increased strength in your calves and quadriceps
- Improvements in vertical leap, lateral shifting, and start speed
- Stimulation of your vestibular system, which improves balance
- Reduced stretch–shortening cycle, which reduces the time it takes the muscles to contract, leading to increases in speed, quickness, power, and improved reaction times
- Increased burning of fat through recruitment of multiple muscle groups and engagement of multiple energy systems
- Improved concentration, which reduces your energy expenditure, increases your endurance, and improves your performance

Aerobic and Anaerobic Training

Rope jumping becomes aerobic and elicits a training response when you perform it for 10 minutes or longer in your aerobic training zone, which is 70 to 80 percent of MHR. But the greatest benefits of jump rope training can be achieved when you use it to develop and train your *anaerobic* energy system. Anaerobic energy systems can boost training zones to 95 percent of MHR and draw upon glucose, rather than oxygen for energy. However, athletes concentrate best on complex tasks when they are in a relaxed mental and physical state that is normally associated with aerobic activities. With the increased oxygenation provided by aerobic fitness, you will be able to sustain concentration for extended periods of time. However, if your goal is to develop speed, explosiveness, and power, it is best to train with high-intensity anaerobic activities, such as my hyperformance jump rope programs.

Once you have developed proper jumping technique and sufficient endurance, your jumping sessions can be performed in the anaerobic training zone (80 to 100 percent of MHR) for 30 to 120 seconds at a time and at $\dot{V}O_2$max from 10 to 30 seconds. In this way, you can achieve maximum benefit in minimal time from a jump rope program tailored to the specific anaerobic energy system intervals of your sport. My programs target the anaerobic energy system to help you develop competitive advantages in the skills discussed in the following sections.

Quickness

Quickness is best understood as reaction time. Good reaction time allows you to take advantage of split-second opportunities to act or react in order to make use of a window of opportunity and thus gain an advantage or recover from a disadvantage. My jump rope training system specifically targets quickness of the hands and feet because most athletic movements are executed by hand, foot, or, in many cases, both. My sprint and circuit training programs, for example, emphasize several sequences of quick hand and foot movements (e.g., in the side swing jump and arm side swing) that can be tailored to match the movement demands of most sports.

Speed

Speed can be defined as quickness sustained over a period of time. Speed is what allows you to maintain and build upon slight advantages, or reduce disadvantages, over distance and time. Speed can be increased and sustained for longer periods by forcing your anaerobic energy system to operate at progressively higher levels of intensity for longer periods of time. My sprint program (see chapter 7) helps you increase speed by challenging your anaerobic energy system to maintain maximum anaerobic intensity for up to 2 minutes. Intensity level is measured by RPM; in other words, higher RPM (up to 300) represents higher intensity. This work will prepare you for the anaerobic demands of any sport.

Agility

Agility is your ability to accelerate, decelerate, and quickly change direction while maintaining your balance, body control, and speed. Agility is very similar to balance in that it forces you to regulate shifts in your body's center of gravity while constantly changing position. Most sports require athletes to move in multiple planes while simultaneously changing direction. My circuit training program (see chapter 9) not only helps you develop quickness in your hands and feet but also enhances your agility by improving your coordination of overall body and foot movements. Greater agility also enables you to make precise changes in direction while moving at high speed.

Explosiveness

Explosiveness is the spark of force that triggers speed. It can be described as force plus quickness. Explosiveness is critical for athletes, such as running backs and wide receivers in American football, who must rapidly reach sprint-level speed in order to achieve or sustain a competitive advantage. It is also crucial to basketball players, who depend on bursts of exertion to leap for rebounds, block shots, and make dunks. My power programs (see chapter 8) are especially designed to help you generate and project explosiveness into critical movements of your sport. They also provide:

- Sustained bouts of anaerobic activity followed by short rest periods
- Simulations of sport-specific movements
- Simulations of the energy demands of your sport
- Establishment of a system to measure your increases in anaerobic capacity and training intensity

Football players rely on explosiveness to give them a performance edge over opponents.

Jump Rope in the Past and Present

Jumping over a rope or ropelike material is one of the oldest forms of recreational activity or exercise. There is evidence that ancient Egyptians and indigenous people of Australia jumped with vines or flexible bamboo. At one time, some cultures used rope jumping as part of a ritual intended to help crops grow. In other cultures, the activity was reserved for males because it was believed that rope jumping would burst the blood vessels in the legs of females. In more modern times, rope jumping evolved from a childhood pastime into a competitive sport; today, double Dutch is being considered as a varsity sport option in some New York public schools.

Rope jumping is known around the world, and each country uses different names to describe the exercise. In the United States, for example, it is called rope jumping or jump rope; in the United Kingdom, Australia, New Zealand, and South Africa it is called skipping; and in Japan it is called *nawatobi*. Regardless of the name, rope jumping is enjoyed around the world. People of all ages enjoy the simple activity of repeatedly jumping over a turning rope. Most people, however, consider it merely a fun activity, something enjoyed primarily by young children and especially by girls. Within this general perception, however, people have different views of rope jumping. Little girls in America may think of the long rope and double Dutch. Boys in elementary school may view rope jumping as something that girls do while singing rhymes. A coach or personal fitness trainer may perceive the jump rope as part of a circuit training workout—a method for warming up the body and a training tool to help athletes improve their sports performance. And others may think of rope jumping as a key component of a boxer's training regimen. For me, rope jumping began as a curiously simple exercise that later evolved into the foundation of my Olympic and military sports training regimens. It continued evolving into the training programs outlined in this book.

3-Step Conditioning Program and Training System

My system consists of a series of steps that will improve your jump rope proficiency and capacity, preparing you for sport-specific jump rope training programs that will enable you to develop your endurance, speed, quickness, agility, and explosiveness (see chapters 6 through 9). Here are the 3 steps:

1. Base phase. Learn the skill of jumping and develop initial jump rope proficiency (see chapter 3).
2. Conditioning phase. Learn the 15 sports training jumps included in level 1, then try the 10 sports training jumps in level 2. Establish basic jump rope capacity (see chapter 4).

3. Sports training phase. Increase your intensity, then establish a baseline to measure your anaerobic fitness levels before beginning the training programs (see chapter 5).

It should take 4 to 6 weeks for most athletes to work through these steps. Each step builds on the previous one and leads to dramatic improvement in targeted athletic capacities. This program is also designed to reduce your risk of injury. By working through these steps, you will be prepared for jump rope training programs that simulate sport-specific movements. These programs also involve intensity and duration levels that simulate the energy system demands of your sport.

I have divided my program into 3 phases to ensure that a wide range of people—from fitness enthusiasts to competitive athletes—can benefit from the challenges at each step of the program. Before learning the 3-step program, you must obtain or gain access to the proper equipment, attire, space, and rope-jumping surface (see chapter 2). These preparations will allow you to enjoy the benefits of rope jumping while reducing your risk of injury. Chapter 2 also discusses how rope jumping can be an extremely portable and effective exercise. For example, several recommended rope-jumping surfaces can be found almost anywhere. In addition, although a high-quality rope is recommended, other options are available to both athletes and fitness enthusiasts. Anyone interested in rope jumping must also be aware of the hazards of using ropes that are made of cable or wire materials or of jumping on concrete, asphalt, or other surfaces that can cause unnecessary stress in the knees and ankles.

The total time you spend in each phase will be determined by your level of physical conditioning and your jump rope proficiency. Once you meet proficiency levels of one phase, you can safely move on to the next. Well-conditioned athletes who have experience with rope jumping may be proficient enough to start at the conditioning phase, assuming that they can meet the performance and proficiency standards of the base phase. Unskilled jumpers and those with poor conditioning should always start with the base phase.

Base Phase

The base phase is the first important step in mastering my system. It teaches you how to jump rope in the correct way—how to master the perfect jump and become proficient in using correct body posture and biomechanics. The purpose of this phase is to prepare you to gradually increase your endurance so that you can add specific techniques introduced in the second, or conditioning, phase.

Conditioning Phase

The conditioning phase prepares you to offset the high-intensity demands of rope jumping. It enables you to take precautions necessary

"Ropenology" (Jump Rope Terminology)

Here are several key terms that will be used throughout the discussions of each phase of my program:

- Continuation—the period of time or number of jumps without interruption, tangles, or catches of the rope
- Duration—the length of training session needed to improve aerobic and anaerobic conditioning
- Frequency—the necessary number of sessions per week to achieve training effects
- Intensity—Level of exertion as measured by energy expended, calories burned, or rope revolutions per minute (RPM) or per second (RPS)
- Baseline—The maximum number of jumps performed in 30 seconds, 60 seconds, or 2 minutes
- "Hyperformance"—A jump roper's ability to perform at high intensity with smooth turning motions, no rope tangles, and free movement in all directions from 180 to 300 RPM (3 to 5 RPS)

for developing basic jump rope capacity and to cultivate a fundamental fitness level that allows your body to adjust to the unique energy system demands of rope jumping. This phase familiarizes you with many rope-jumping techniques that you will use throughout the rest of the training program. You will learn how to jump rope at different intensity levels while using a variety of movements that simulate those of various sports. It may take a couple of weeks or longer for you to become comfortable with many of these techniques, but it is important that you take your time. As you go through the next steps in the program, you will find that it is important to establish many of these techniques as second nature—that is, part of your muscle memory—because you will learn how to combine them in novel ways to increase your fitness levels while also making substantial leaps in quickness, balance, agility, speed, and power.

The conditioning phase also prepares you for the strenuous demands of phase 3—the sports training phase—in which you combine techniques learned in the conditioning phase at intensity levels designed to help you develop the capacity for sustained anaerobic power. In other words, the sports training phase helps you develop the capacity to jump up to 240+ RPM for 2 minutes. This intensity requires most athletes to push themselves to 95 percent or higher of their maximum heart rate. As a result, it is best to make sure that you progress successfully through the base and conditioning phases before undertaking the sports training phase. If you attempt the third phase prematurely, you may suffer injury or undue physical strain.

Sports Training Phase

The sports training phase is especially designed for the serious competitive athlete who wants to incorporate all of my jump rope techniques into a training program that continues to build anaerobic conditioning and the full range of competitive benefits of each of my techniques. The sports training phase includes everything from the bounce step to power jumping. Durations can be as short as 30 seconds to several minutes. The sports training phase demands that you virtually master all of the jump rope techniques, possess the capacity to jump continuously for 10 minutes or more, and maintain high-intensity levels (i.e., 95 percent of MHR) for extended durations in several sets per workout session.

The sports training phase also helps you develop the anaerobic fitness levels necessary to execute the refined movements of my advanced jump rope training programs. You will develop a baseline (see chapter 5) to establish intensity levels necessary for starting the advanced training programs upon completing the 3 phases described in chapters 3, 4, and 5.

Comparing Rope Jumping
With Other Exercises

My system combines anaerobic conditioning with simulations of sport-specific movements to generate dramatic improvement in sports performance. Table 1.1 shows that rope jumping performed at a low intensity of 120 RPM produces cardiovascular benefits.

Table 1.1   Exercise Comparison Chart

Jumping rope for 10 minutes at 120 RPM produces the same cardiovascular fitness as the following activities:	
Activity	**Time**
Cycling	2 miles in 6 minutes
Handball	20 minutes
Jogging	30 minutes at a moderate pace
Running	1 mile in 12 minutes
Swimming	720 yards in 12 minutes
Tennis	2 sets

Rope jumping also provides a good option for athletes seeking a fat-burning or fitness program. Rope jumping offers greater fat-burning benefits than do most cardiovascular activities that emphasize lower-body muscle groups because it incorporates muscle groups and joints of the lower and upper body. As a result, a 160-pound (73-kilogram) person jumping rope at an average speed of 120 RPM burns approximately 12.9 calories per minute or 720 calories per hour (see table 1.2). Calories expended are determined by body weight; therefore a heavier athlete burns more calories at the same intensity level and duration of rope jumping.

Jump rope is nearly as effective as running in burning calories. But when certain arm and foot movements are added to a jumping session, its fat-burning value increases substantially. To burn away extra pounds, athletes can jump at 120 to 140 RPM. Combining this exercise with proper diet and rest can produce noticeable fat loss, as well as fitness gains, in mere weeks.

I have trained thousands of athletes for fitness and sports performance. Rope jumping as a training method is effective because it can improve your dynamic balance, your efficiency of movement, and your skills in a specific sport. The rest of this book explains in greater detail how you can use jump rope training to improve your fitness or sports performance. Along the way, I answer such questions as the following: *What is the correct way to jump? How do I develop my jump rope capacity? How do I learn different techniques? How should I jump for my sport?* Whether you are a coach or an athlete, I want you to walk away from this book with a greater understanding of rope jumping and its potential to boost fitness and performance.

Jump Rope Training in MMA

Amir Sadollah, an amateur fighter from the Combat Sports Center in Richmond, Virginia, rose from obscurity to fame by winning the 2008 *Ultimate Fighter 7* mixed martial arts (MMA) tournament televised by Spike TV. A student of Sifu Brian Crenshaw, Sadollah became the Cinderella man of the Ultimate Fighting Championship (UFC), as with no prior professional fights he defeated all pros to earn his first UFC contract. Amir reports that the Buddy Lee jump rope training system has proven to be a key part of his overall training regimen; in fact, he says that rope jumping has made the winning difference by enabling him to achieve key advantages in speed, quickness, agility, and explosiveness—even as he develops a level of fitness superior to that of his opponents. Today, Amir shares this rope system with other fighters at MMA legend Randy Couture's gym, including UFC champions such as Forrest Griffin.

Table 1.2 Energy Expenditure by a 160-Pound (73-Kilogram) Person

Activity	Calories burned per minute
Light	
Cleaning, light (dusting, picking up)	3.2
Shopping	2.9
Sitting	1.9
Sleeping	1.1
Moderate	
Badminton	5.7
Bicycling at 10 miles (16 km) per hour	5.1
Bowling	3.8
Canoeing	5.1
Gardening	5.7
Golf with no cart	5.7
Kayaking	6.4
Swimming (treading water)	5.1
Walking at 3 miles (4.8 km) per hour	4.2
Hard	
Aerobic dance (high impact)	8.9
Chopping wood	7.7
Skating (roller or ice)	8.9
Skiing downhill with moderate effort	7.7
Tennis (doubles)	7.7
Walking with backpack	8.9
Very hard	
Cross-country skiing	11.5
Handball	15.3
Jumping rope (at 120 RPM)	12.9
Rowing with vigorous effort	15.3
Running at 10 minutes per mile (1.6 km)	12.8

Adapted, by permission, from S.N. Blair, A.L. Dunn, B.H. Marcus, et al., 2001, *Active living every day* (Champaign, IL: Human Kinetics), 179-182. Based on selected MET values created by B.E. Ainsworth, W.L. Haskell, M.C. Whitt, et al., 2000, "Compendium of Physical Activities: An update of activity codes and MET intensities," *Medicine & Science in Sports & Exercise* 32(9): S498-S516.

Get Ready to Jump

Even though rope jumping is a simple and portable exercise, you must take reasonable precautions and certain preparatory steps to allow yourself to get the most out of the experience. This chapter will help you do so. It shows you three keys to getting the most out of your 5- to 10-minute jump rope training sessions: proper form, posture, and understanding of three particular rope adjustments. It also shows you how to maximize your benefits while reducing your injury risk by making good choices about jumping surface, equipment, and attire. You'll get the most out of your jump rope training if you wear clothes that allow free movement, do your training on surfaces that absorb impact *and* provide natural rebound effects, and use ropes designed to facilitate quickness, speed, and continuation. It is also important that you learn how to properly store your rope in order to preserve its usefulness and ensure its functionality and overall quality of performance.

Warming Up

To avoid injury while jumping rope, it is very important that you warm up. The following stretches and movements are good ways to warm up the major muscle groups you will use while jumping. The primary areas to focus on during your warm-up are your feet, calves, and ankles.

Ankle Stretches

One great way to warm up your ankles is to perform "ankle alphabets," a technique used by many dancers and gymnasts. When doing "ankle alphabets," either sit or stand, and starting with the right foot, try to trace each letter of the alphabet in cursive using the toes. You will notice your ankle rolling in variety of directions as you trace each letter. After completing the alphabet on the right foot, repeat with the left foot. Try making each letter of the alphabet with each foot.

Calf Stretches

Stretching your Achilles tendon and calf muscle helps you maintain elasticity in the tendon in order to avoid tendonitis. Women who wear high heels, along with anyone who stands for long hours, will tend to have tighter calf muscles and thus should take particular care to perform calf stretching prior to jumping rope. Two types of calf stretches are appropriate:

1. Standing calf stretch. Begin by facing a wall, standing two feet away. Place your hands against the wall, step back with one leg, and bend the front knee. Gently press the heel of the back foot down to stretch the gastrocnemius muscle. Hold the stretch for 30 seconds. Then bend your back knee and gently press that heel to the ground to stretch the soleus muscle. Hold for 30 seconds. Repeat on the other leg.

2. Seated calf stretch. Sit with both legs extended and place a belt or towel around both feet. Pull the belt or towel with both hands, flexing both feet to feel a stretch in the back of your legs. Keeping your back flat, slowly lower your chest to your legs. Hold for 30 seconds.

Peroneal Stretches

The peroneal muscles in your lower legs stabilize and strengthen your ankles when you jump. If these muscles get overworked and are not stretched, you may experience tendonitis. To perform the stretch, place a belt or towel around one foot. Lie on your back so that your leg is extended above you. Pull with both hands to feel the stretch in your calf muscle. Hold that stretch and gently pull with your inside arm, supinating your foot (i.e., turning it inward). You should now feel a stretch on the outside of your leg; these are your peroneal muscles. Hold the stretch 30 seconds, and then repeat with the other leg.

Common Injuries Due to Incorrect Technique

Sore calves and shin splints are the most common injuries experienced by rope jumpers, and they usually result either from excessive jumping in the beginner phase or from improper foot placement when jumping. In addition, the calf muscle is the primary muscle acting on the foot during rope jumping, thus explaining the common complaint of muscle soreness in that area. You can avoid calf muscle fatigue, however, by adequately stretching after you jump rope.

Shin splints are associated with excessive jumping for the beginner and with jumping flat-footed or with improper foot placement. Your tibialis posterior muscle controls the movement of your foot in the transverse plane, and overworking this muscle results in shin splints. You can prevent shin splints by placing your feet properly (i.e., keeping them parallel to each other) when jumping and by avoiding surfaces that do not give good rebound (e.g., concrete). To avoid strain of the posterior tibialis muscle remember to land on the ball of the foot to avoid fully loading the foot and heel.

Improper handling of the rope can also contribute to injury. If you perform with excessive turning movements or use an overly tight grip, you may experience soreness in your shoulders, forearms, or hands. These are common mistake among novice jumpers, who spend too much energy trying to coordinate the rope swing with the jump instead of relaxing and breathing correctly. Remember to hold the rope with a firm but gentle grip by placing a handle in each hand between your thumb and index finger while wrapping your hand around the barrel of the rope.

Plantar fasciitis or pain under the heel can result from jumping too high, landing with high impact, or jumping excessively without adequate calf stretching. This ailment is commonly resolved through stretching of the calves and massage of the plantar fascia or arch of the foot. If you experience pain in the arch when jumping, allow adequate recovery time before you resume rope jumping in order to avoid overstrain and inflammation of the plantar fascia.

Tendonitis (inflammation of a tendon) is common as an overuse injury when jumping rope. To avoid tendon injury, thoroughly warm up your feet and ankles before jumping rope and take time to stretch after you jump. Peroneal tendonitis is a common injury when a person jumps with the feet turned out (abducted). Jumping in this way overworks the peroneal muscles, instead of using the stronger calf muscles, and thus leads to inflammation of the peroneal tendons. For optimal foot function when jumping, focus on parallel foot placement.

Injuries Related to Rope Jumping

Most jump-rope-related injuries occur either in the early stages of learning to jump or when jumping with incorrect technique. The injuries involve a number of factors that can easily be corrected with proper instruction. Two incorrect techniques involve jumping too high and landing incorrectly on a hard surface; the key here is to jump with good posture and use your lower body to absorb impact. Injury can also be caused by attempting to jump at high levels of intensity before achieving the appropriate level of conditioning. Some people jump too much too soon—for example, by engaging in my jump rope training programs or in nonstop sessions exceeding 10 minutes before they have mastered my 3-step jump rope training program presented in chapters 3, 4, and 5. The risk here is the same as in resistance training. Too much too soon can cause injury. Remember that safety should be the first consideration in any jump rope program.

Common Mistakes Leading to Injury

- Incorrect measurement of the rope
- Jumping too high or landing incorrectly (flat-footed or on the heels)
- Jumping on hard surfaces (e.g., concrete, cement)
- Jumping too much too soon (before acquiring sufficient technique and endurance)
- Jumping with loose jewelry, hair, shoelaces, clothes
- Gripping the handles too tightly
- Making large circles with the rope handles when turning the rope
- Jumping on a surface that is not clear of debris
- Jumping in a crowded space with people passing by or exercising nearby
- Attempting advanced or extreme jumping techniques without mastery of fundamentals

Rope jumping is a skill movement that requires you to learn proper technique and timing and good biomechanics in order to become proficient. Jump-rope-related injury is inevitable when one does not approach this exercise with patience, regular practice, and safe progression.

In general, when an injury occurs, the athlete should rest and refrain from jumping. Ice therapy is effective in treating most jump-rope-related injuries. Apply an ice pack to the injury with an elastic wrap (20 minutes on and 30 minutes off). Continue this pattern for the next few hours. During this time, the injured body part should be elevated so that it is higher than the heart. Treating injuries in this manner helps decrease swelling and promotes blood flow back to the heart. Injury can also be avoided by warming up the feet, ankles, and lower extremities by means of stretching exercises (see chapter 11), by jumping on proper surfaces, and by using correct jumping form.

Here are some guidelines for preventing jump-rope-related injuries:

- **Stretch.** Before and after each jump rope session, stretch to prevent injury and muscle soreness. Taking at least 20 minutes to stretch before and after an exercise session can reduce discomfort, especially that caused by delayed muscle soreness. Stretching can also reduce your risk of muscle pulls and muscle strains. In addition, a flexible muscle is a strong muscle; therefore, stretching can improve performance and endurance. It is especially important to stretch your calves. Stretching guidelines can be found in chapter 11.

- **Check your jump rope.** Ensure that it is properly sized for your height and that the cord and connection device (ball and swivel bearings, eyelets) are secured. It is critical to verify that these components do not come apart and cause injury.

- **Jump on a proper surface.** Good options include a suspended wooden floor, artificial turf, and rubberized surfaces. Also wear cross-training shoes with forefoot padding to absorb impact, and remember to progress slowly (take plenty of time to master the skill of jumping).

- **Be patient.** First master the two basic jump rope techniques. Do not rush to learn the 25 techniques presented in chapter 4.

- **Focus.** Be aware of your immediate surroundings and space. Observe people and objects that may interfere with the path of your rope and thus cause facial or bodily injury to you or others. Jump rope speeds can reach 80 to 100 miles (about 130–160 km) per hour.

- **Rest.** The need for rest is underappreciated by many athletes, but it is during periods of rest that the body makes fitness and performance gains. During rest, muscle fibers are repaired, which results in increased ability to perform at high levels. Periods of rest also allow your brain to process and integrate new information, such as an innovative sports techniques or performance strategies. Athletes may find that after a short period of rest (perhaps 1 or 2 days) their body has recovered from training or performance, and they possess an improved ability to execute a sports movement or performance strategy that has been recently incorporated into their training program.

Common Injuries and Solutions

Shin Splints or Sore Calves

Symptom: Inflammation of tendons and muscles of the shin brought on by the impact forces of exercise.

Cause: Common sports injury usually resulting from excessive jumping during the beginner's phase or from a long layoff; can also result from gaining too much weight or jumping on surfaces (e.g., concrete) that are too hard and do not provide sufficient give or rebound.

Treatment: Stop jumping at first sign of pain; continued jumping will irritate or aggravate the injury. Massage with ice for 20 minutes to reduce inflammation. Consult with your physician or athletic trainer, who may suggest taking an anti-inflammatory medication to reduce swelling.

Prevention: Raise body temperature first, then stretch calves by walking on your heels. Progress slowly with jumping and train on an appropriate surface (e.g., level dirt or grass, rubberized mat, artificial turf) to minimize shin trauma.

Plantar Fasciitis

Symptom: Irritation and swelling of the thick tissue on the bottom of the foot (pain under the heel); involves mild swelling, redness, and tenderness on the bottom of the heel or along the outside border of the heel. Can last from several months to a couple of years.

Cause: Usually results from overuse or incorrect landing on the outside of the heel, especially if you have high-arched feet; can also result from jumping too high or landing flat-footed or with high impact in the early phases of rope jumping.

Treatment: Recovery techniques include heel stretching exercises, shoe inserts, and anti-inflammatory medications. Consult your doctor or athletic trainer for a recovery program.

Prevention: Good stretching improves flexibility around the ankle; stretching the Achilles tendon and calf muscles is considered an effective way to prevent plantar fasciitis.

Sore Forearms

Symptom: Irritation and swelling of the flexors located in the upper region of the forearm.

Cause: Overly tight gripping of the rope handle during jumping sessions.

Treatment: Decrease the duration of jumping and use ice to reduce inflammation.

Prevention: Do not grip the handles too tightly; grasp them between your thumb and index finger with a firm yet soft grip. When jumping, rotate the rope handles with small circular movements. Stretch your forearms before and after jump training sessions.

Surface and Training Area

The best surfaces for rope jumping provide rebound during the take-off phase of each jump and sufficient absorption for the landing phase. These high-quality surfaces help you develop speed, quickness, and explosive power. Avoid jumping on concrete, which increases your risk of injury. Concrete may absorb impact, but it does not provide the rebound effect that improves your performance and reduces your risk of lower-body injury. This risk is similar to those entailed in running, jogging, and sprinting on concrete, asphalt, and similar surfaces. Recommended hard surfaces include the following:

- Rubberized gym floor or mat
- Well-manicured grass
- Wooden floor
- Artificial turf
- Carpeted surface
- Tennis court (clay)
- Gymnastics floor (spring surface)
- Level dirt (baseball infield)
- Padded mats

You should consider using a soft surface only after you have mastered rope jumping on a hard surface. Soft surfaces (e.g., some exercise mats) may absorb impact, but they require extra effort and energy during the takeoff phase of each jump. This extra effort can help you develop leg, knee, and ankle strength while minimizing your risk of injury; in fact, this minimizing of injury risk allows athletes and fitness enthusiasts who are recovering from knee or other leg injuries to train on soft surfaces (e.g., rubber mats). You should, however, limit jumping sets in this situation to somewhere between 10 and 60 seconds. If you want to use a soft surface, I recommend that you use a wrestling mat, a judo mat, or well-manicured grass.

Once you select a proper surface, identify an appropriate jump rope training area that meets the following clearance criteria (also see figure 2.1).

- 2 feet (0.6 m) or more above your head
- 5 feet (1.5 m) in front of your body
- 5 feet behind your body
- 3 feet (0.9 m) beyond the distance of each extended arm

Figure 2.1   The jump rope training area should extend 2 feet (0.6 m) above your head and 3 feet (0.9 m) beyond the length of each extended arm.

Shoes and Attire

Because rope jumping requires you to bounce and balance your body weight on the balls of your feet, choose a pair of cross-training shoes with ample forefoot padding. For other clothing, as a general guideline, wear the athletic or training gear that you normally use when practicing or training for your sport. Note the following considerations:

- Do not wear baggy clothing or attire that can come apart, drop to the floor, or otherwise distract you while you execute jump rope movements. Extremely loose attire increases your risk of tripping and suffering injury.
- Do not wear hats, jewelry, or other accessories that can fall from your body while you jump; these accessories also increase your risk of tripping and getting injured.
- Make sure that your shoestrings are properly laced.
- If you have long hair, tie it back or pin it down to prevent it from interfering with the swing of the rope.

- If you are a woman, wear a good support bra.
- Wear a headband and wristbands to prevent heavy perspiration from getting into your eyes or on the rope's handles or swivel bearings. Moisture can cause you to lose your grip or even let go of the rope, thus increasing your risk of personal injury while also possibly endangering others who are training or watching nearby.

Ropes

Train with the rope that best allows you to jump for fitness or best simulates the speed, quickness, and agility demands of your sport. One decision you face in choosing a rope is whether to use a lightweight rope or a heavier one. A lightweight, aerodynamic speed rope responds easily to directional change with minimal air resistance. In contrast, heavy ropes provide upper-body plyometric workouts but do not effectively increase quickness of the hands and feet. A jump rope training program is best used for developing speed, quickness, agility, and explosiveness, and a lightweight speed rope enables you to maximize these and other benefits of jump rope training.

The best choice is a speed rope made with flexible PVC (polyvinyl chloride) plastic that easily turns at 180 to 300 revolutions per minute (RPM) or 3 to 5 revolutions per second (RPS). Ropes made of cable rod or metallic materials can also attain high speeds, but they pose a strong risk of serious injury to you and to passersby during high-intensity rope training. PVC is the most versatile rope material available because it can be tailored to the ideal weight and thickness that maximizes the rope's aerodynamic properties. These features allow you to generate the highest possible number of repetitions per jump rope set, and the training programs presented in this book take advantage of the aerodynamic properties of the PVC speed rope. This kind of rope also allows you to perform extended periods of continuation (i.e., successive jumps between catches of the rope), which is another important principle in my jump rope training system because it maximizes rope jumping benefits.

Admittedly, there has not been a standardization of rope jumping materials in terms of qualities such as weight, measurement, and thickness. However, because of almost four decades of rope jumping experience, I have learned that PVC cords are the best rope jumping material on the market. Ropes made of slow-turning materials, such as cotton or lightweight leather, turn at a top speed of 2 RPS, which is not fast enough to help you develop high levels of quickness and speed. A slow-turning rope also forces you to expend extra effort in order to compensate for the rope's drag through the air; this, in turn, reduces your number of repetitions per set and your periods of continuation, thus making it difficult for you to get the most out of my jump rope training program.

Unskilled jumpers, however, may have difficulty coordinating the rope swing and should choose initially to master the basic jump rope skills by using a thicker, slower-turning cord that comfortably turns at 120 RPM or 2 RPS. Unfortunately, the packaging of most jump ropes does not include information about RPM or RPS; many are commercial products designed to meet general fitness needs of the general public. Thus it is up to you to understand that those jump ropes designed specifically to maximize rope jumping benefits are usually the speed ropes made with PVC. In contrast, heavy ropes (which are generally described or marketed as such) are best used to increase upper-body strength and endurance rather than to enhance speed or quickness. These ropes can be used in conjunction with speed ropes to perform a fortified jump rope training program, but you must first achieve mastery of basic rope jumping skills. As your basic skills increase, so will your need for a high-quality speed rope that enables the high RPM levels that challenge your anaerobic energy systems.

Use table 2.1 to compare different types of ropes. I recommend any of the "hyperformance" speed ropes because they have a patented, external, swivel-ball-bearing system that virtually eliminates the friction, drag, and wear associated with other jump ropes. These properties allow for ultrafast turning action, omnidirectional movement, and better control, all of which enables you to improve your hand and foot speed. In addition, the ropes' handles and total weight are designed for a comfortable fit and feel for both children and adults.

A hyperformance rope's swivel-ball-bearing wrench can be used to secure and replace the swivel bearings in order to optimize the rope's performance. This innovative adjustment system enables you to adjust the rope to your height in seconds by cutting the cord to the desired length and twisting it back into the handle. The adjustment system also allows you to easily replace the aerodynamic PVC rope cord. The balancing properties of the aerodynamic rope cord enable you to better control your rope swings and quickly master basic rope jumping skills. The swivel bearings, rope cords, and foam grips are replaceable. Remember—a training program is ineffective without high-quality equipment, and my hyperformance ropes have proven themselves when put to use by athletes at all levels. "Buddy's ropes turn so quickly that you are forced to move your feet and hands much faster than you would using a conventional rope," says Burton Richardson, leading authority on martial artist Bruce Lee's Jeet Kune Do concepts and columnist for *Inside Kung-Fu* magazine. "This enhances agility and cardiovascular conditioning and is great fun. If it wasn't the very best equipment I have used, I wouldn't recommend it." For more information on hyperformance jump rope equipment, see www.buddyleejumpropes.com.

Table 2.1 Rope Comparison Chart

Rope type	Performance
Leather rope	The leather rope has been around for almost a century and is well known in the boxing world. It is simple to construct and relatively durable. However, too much energy is wasted on the effort to turn the rope. This energy should be concentrated on foot speed. The leather rope does turn more efficiently than beaded, nylon, cotton, and heavy ropes, but it does not compare to a speed rope in producing lightning-fast reflexes. Leather ropes also wear and fray over time and are susceptible to deterioration when exposed to water. In addition, the leather rope usually is not adjustable, which forces you to either make wide circles with your wrists in compensation for extra rope length or crouch over to accommodate a rope that's too short; this posture promotes improper form and increases risk of injury. If you do use a leather rope, try to buy it in a size that is close to your ideal rope length. (This recommendation applies for all ropes that cannot be adjusted.)
Licorice speed rope	This thick-cord PVC rope is a good basic speed rope for learning the skill of jumping. There is no standard thickness, and you can easily determine why this rope has a limited capacity for high-intensity performance by quickly testing it before purchase. It shares the durability of relatively thinner PVC cord ropes, but it may not turn fast enough to help you develop the reaction times and speed that generate competitive advantages in most sports. Most of these ropes are not adjustable but can be shortened by tying knots near the handles.
Cable rope	Ropes made with cable and cable-like materials can turn quickly, especially if the rope is made of thin, woven cable rod. These ropes are not very elastic, however, and may not allow you to use many of the jump rope techniques in this book. They can best be used for speed jumping—not for arm-cross movements or advanced jumping. Many of them break very easily, which means you may have to replace them on a regular basis if you undertake an aggressive and frequent jump rope training routine. They are not adjustable. In addition, cable ropes pose the greatest risk of injury to self and others when the jumper misses while jumping at a high speed.
Beaded rope	A beaded rope consists of plastic segmented links threaded onto a thin cotton cord. This hard plastic rope is common in elementary schools and is designed for outdoor jumping on cement. Depending upon the heaviness of the beads, it can provide a balanced weight that turns easily for athletes or fitness enthusiasts at novice or beginner levels of rope jumping. It will not, however, improve your hand or foot speed. What's more, this type of rope becomes hazardous when the rope cord, especially the plastic links, begin to wear or break; if the cord breaks, segmented parts can fly in several directions. You may be able to adjust the rope cord by untying a small knot in the handle, removing the necessary beads, cutting the rope, and tying a new knot.

(continued)

29

Table 2.1 *(continued)*

Rope type	Performance
Cotton or nylon rope	Cotton and nylon ropes turn very poorly and create excessive drag. Therefore, they are not functional for sports cross-training. Regardless of how quickly you turn your wrists, these ropes won't respond fast enough to provide significant training benefits. They are usually not adjustable and are the most inefficient of all ropes.
Heavy rope	Heavy ropes are commonly thought to help develop upper-body strength. These ropes may be made with hard rubber or plastic; some of them use what can be described as more standard rope materials while providing the effect of a weighted rope by adding weight to the rope handles. However, heavy ropes, whether weighted in the rope material itself or in the handles, can cause excessive upper-body stress when used by unskilled or unfit jumpers. Safer and more effective ways to develop upper-body strength include resistance training and calisthenics; you can also use a medicine ball for upper-body training. A heavy rope is not adjustable and will not improve hand or foot speed.
"Hyperformance" swivel-ball-bearing speed ropes	
Buddy Lee's Aero Speed Rope	This short-handled rope is suitable for high-intensity speed and power jumping. It is recommended for adults and for children of age 8 or older. It has an externally mounted swivel bearing system that promotes unmatched speed, no rope tangle, and minimum friction and drag.
Buddy Lee's Rope Master Rope	This long-handled rope can be used for speed and power and for developing intricate hand and foot movements (e.g., arm, leg, and body crosses). It is recommended for adults and for children of age 8 or older. It has an externally mounted swivel bearing system that promotes unmatched speed, no rope tangle, and minimum friction and drag.
Buddy Lee's Junior Speed Rope	This short-handled rope is suitable for high-intensity speed and power jumping. It is recommended for adults and for children of age 8 or older. It has an externally mounted swivel bearing system that promotes unmatched speed, no rope tangle, and minimum friction and drag.

Rope Measurements

There are three rope measurements, each of which emphasizes different training effects: distance from jumping surface to shoulder, distance from jumping surface to underarm, and distance from jumping surface to upper chest. If you are a beginner, start with the surface-to-shoulder measurement in order to ensure sufficient clearance over your head as you learn basic jumping skills. Once you become better conditioned and more proficient—and thus use more streamlined movements—you can shorten the rope to the next level (i.e., distance from the jumping surface to your underarm) to achieve greater benefits through increased recruitment of muscle fibers. Doing so will enable you to gain an even greater competitive edge. When you use a shorter rope, you have less room for error and are forced to move your hands and feet faster, which dramatically increases rotational speed. This process increases your whole-body awareness, helps you develop lightning-fast reflexes, and improves your reaction time.

If you become aware that your jump rope is smacking against the jumping surface, it is time to shorten the rope. Eventually, if you become an experienced jumper who makes very little wasted movement, you can move on to the next rope measurement—from jumping surface to upper chest. You may also need to use measurements between the standard levels of shoulder, underarm, upper chest. The most preferred measurement is the underarm measurement. Not all jumpers will reach a level of proficiency where it makes sense to use the lower chest measurement.

Here are three guidelines to follow when considering whether to shorten your rope length:

1. Do not consider shortening your rope before you have met the fitness and skill criteria of your current training phase.
2. Determine whether shortening your rope will help you best simulate the movement and energy demands of your sport.
3. If you intend to use the rope as part of several training regimens, it may be best to shorten it by creating small knots that can be let out later, rather than making permanent adjustments (in which the rope is cut and screwed into the swivel).

I suggest that you use the following three rope lengths for sports cross-training. Each length allows you to increase your training intensity, thus improving your foot speed, conditioning, and reflexes (reaction time). Regardless of which length you use, it is important that you maintain correct rope jumping form. Proper form is the key to achieving the rope jumping speeds and intensity levels that lead you to high levels of fitness and sports performance.

Shoulder Measurement: 12-Inch (30 cm) Clearance

A rope length equal to the distance from the jumping surface to your shoulder is ideal for mastering the 15 basic jumping techniques and can enable you to produce up to 200 RPM (3.3 RPS). A rope adjusted at shoulder height will clear your head by about a foot (30 cm) as you execute basic jump rope movements (see figure 2.2). As you become more proficient at jumping, you can reduce your rope length so that the rope clears your head by 6 to 10 inches (15 to 25 cm) during high-speed jump rope training sessions. As noted earlier, consider carefully whether making such an adjustment will simulate the movement and energy demands of your sport better than the shoulder measurement does.

To use the shoulder measurement to determine your proper rope length, follow these steps.

1. Stand on the center of the rope with one foot.
2. Pull the handles up along the side of your body so that the tips of the handles extend no higher than your shoulder (see figure 2.2a). If the handles extend beyond your shoulders, the rope is too long, which will cause excessive drag through the air, reduce the rope's rotational speed, and increase the frequency of catches and tangles. These effects, in turn, will reduce your duration of continuation, even if you are using a lightweight speed rope.

If the rope is too long, adjust the length by temporarily tying knots in the rope. Though it may slightly reduce your rope-jumping efficiency, you may need to tie more than one knot on each side in order to establish the proper rope-jumping length. Once you become comfortable with the proper rope length, take out the knots and make a permanent adjustment to an appropriate rope length. Avoid cutting the rope too short, since doing so may force you to purchase another rope.

Underarm Measurement: 10-Inch (25 cm) Clearance

Once you master the initial two basic techniques and build a basic jump rope capacity (see chapter 3), you can shorten your rope to the next length (to the underarm) for better rope performance. At this measurement, you will be able to feel that the rope is now turning faster. This rope measurement is perhaps the most used and most comfortable among jump rope enthusiasts.

Upper Chest Measurement: 6-Inch (15 cm) Clearance

This rope measurement, which extends from your feet to your upper chest (see figure 2.3), is used when one becomes very proficient and is used primarily by highly skilled and advanced jumpers. It involves a rope clearance of only a couple of inches over the head during jumping. It is

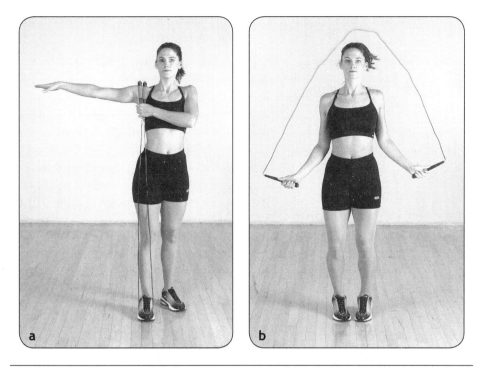

Figure 2.2 (*a*) For the shoulder measurement, extend the rope to your shoulder. (*b*) The shoulder-based rope length provides good clearance.

Figure 2.3 Upper chest measurement.

TIP

If your rope excessively smacks the surface with each pass or clears your head by more than a foot (30 cm), then it is too long. Remember that the standard length is a guideline, not an exact measurement for all individuals.

a length used among athletes who have become proficient in the sports training jumps and have increased their jump rope capacity to 5 to 10 minutes. Before using this length, you should have completed my 3-step system and become an accomplished jumper so that you can appreciate the faster turns prompted by the shorter rope length. This will be your preferred length when doing hyperformance jump rope training programs in order to get the best training benefits from each jump session. This length is best for producing jump speeds up to 4 RPS.

Lower Chest Measurement: 4-Inch (10 cm) Clearance

For very advanced jumpers, a rope that extends from the feet to the bottom of the rib cage enables the fastest rope speeds for sports cross-training without sacrificing proper body posture and technique (see figure 2.4). Ropes so short that they reach only to the hips or lower abdomi-

Figure 2.4 (*a*) Lower chest measurement. (*b*) Rope clearance with the lower chest measurement.

nals are generally used only by competitive and world-class jumpers. This rope length should be avoided because it compromises correct rope jumping form and may take many years of training to use safely. My jump rope training system is not designed to prepare you for jump rope competitions; rather, it teaches you how to cross-train at different rope lengths in order to improve your cardiovascular fitness and athletic skills.

Rope Care

Take good care of your rope in order to maximize your training benefits. First, store it properly after each training session. Leaving your rope in very hot or cold temperatures can break or alter the shape of the PVC rope material. Second, let the rope hang from a hook, a door, or a coat rack when not in use. Wrapping the rope around its handles will create tangles that may not straighten out for thousands of revolutions. This problem can waste time, negatively influence your training, and reduce the training life of your rope.

Buddy Lee Jump Rope Checklist

1. Always read the rope's instructions.
2. Adjust your rope properly for your height and skill level.
3. To ensure safety, check the rope cord, handles, and turning mechanisms for breakage or unsecured parts before each jumping session.
4. Select a recommended jumping surface in order to minimize impact and avoid lower-body injuries.
5. Remove loose objects and debris from the jumping surface.
6. Stay hydrated during rope jumping sessions. Proper hydration allows you to train at higher intensity levels and for longer durations. It also helps you maintain the close concentration demanded by jump rope training.
7. Remove jewelry, tie back long hair, and make sure to securely tie your shoes before your jump rope session. During your training breaks, wear the rope around your shoulders. This ensures keeping track of your rope, avoids mix-ups, and makes it easier to resume jump rope training.
8. After each jumping session, store your jump rope loosely in a gym bag or hang it over a hook. Do not wrap the cord around the handles; doing so may create kinks in the rope that interfere with its performance.
9. Store your rope at room temperature. Avoid cold, damp, or hot spaces that may cause premature breakage or deterioration of rope materials.

Step 1: Base Phase—Master the Basic Techniques

The base phase teaches you how to jump correctly. It reveals my secrets for performing the perfect jump and mastering the two basic techniques that lay the foundation for all of the jump rope skills used in my training system. These two basic jumps are the basic bounce and the alternate-foot step. You will repeat these perfect jumps hundreds of times per session, thus enhancing your proficiency and building your endurance so that you can master more advanced techniques. The base phase gives you a step-by-step program in which you will develop a basic jump rope proficiency of 140 consecutive jumps for each technique, then build up to a continuation of 500 jumps that ensures you are prepared for the next (conditioning) phase of my training system.

Biomechanics of Rope Jumping

Rope jumping involves three phases in each jump—load phase, flight phase, and landing phase—and you will perform each of these phases hundreds of times during each jumping session. The *load phase* requires you to balance your body on the balls of your feet with your knees slightly flexed. The *flight phase* consists of muscular contractions that propel your body high enough to clear the rope with each jump. In the *landing phase*, you return to the surface by allowing your body weight to balance on the balls of your feet with your knees flexed to help absorb the impact of the landing. Efficient recovery from the landing phase through the load phase to the flight phase is critical if you are going to enjoy the benefits of jump rope training.

Load Phase

Your body weight should be balanced on the balls of your feet, and your knees should be slightly bent in an upright version of the universal athletic position discussed in chapter 1. This position prepares your body for the multijoint demands of rope jumping. Ideally, you should jump no higher than 1/2 to 3/4 of an inch (1.3 to 1.9 cm) from the jumping surface (the exception to this rule involves power jumping, which is discussed later in the book). This approach leaves you virtually no room for error and therefore reinforces your performance of precise movements. Jumping in this manner—rising less than an inch from the surface and landing lightly on the balls of your feet—requires you to exercise concentration, kinesthetic awareness, and perfect timing. This is a refined and highly skilled whole-body movement. Many people find that it is relatively easy to "give it all you've got" when asked to jump or leap, but it is quite a different matter to jump with control. In rope jumping, less is more. See figure 3.1 for a diagram of the muscles worked during this phase.

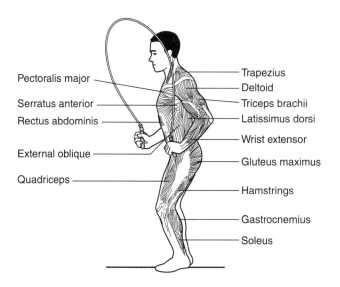

Figure 3.1 Muscles used during the load phase.

Flight Phase

The flight phase consists of two stages: the propulsion stage and the airborne stage. Understanding what happens from the moment your feet push off the surface to the point when you are in the air is critical to maximizing your training benefits and reducing your risk of injury. You generate propulsion by means of a slight push from your ankles, calves, knees, and hips. Push through the jump rope surface from the balls of your feet and point your toes toward the surface as you become airborne (see figure 3.2a).

During the airborne phase, your feet should rise no more than 1 inch (2.5 cm) from the surface as the rope passes under your feet. Swinging the rope and jumping over it recruits muscles in your upper and lower body (see figure 3.2b). This movement is essential to enhancing your proprioception in your feet and ankles, so that you know where to plant your feet and how to balance so you don't topple over. Proprioception, known as an inner sense, is the ability of your central nervous system to communicate and coordinate parts of your body with each other. This movement also increases your balance, rhythm, and timing, while reducing your risk of injury. Repetition of these movements improves your body's kinesthetic awareness (known as the outer sense, the body's awareness of where it is in space and time) or the body's ability to coordinate motion knowing where the rope is in relationship to the body during jumping.

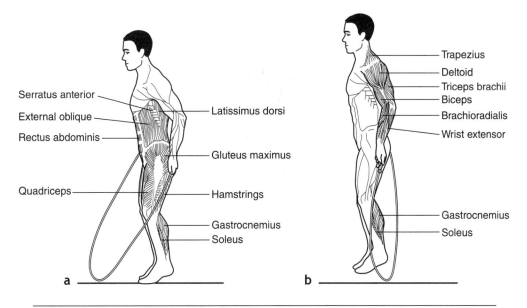

Figure 3.2 Muscles used during the (a) propulsion and (b) airborne stages of the flight phase.

Landing Phase

Your shock-absorbing joints (i.e., your knees, ankles, and hips) diffuse the impact of each landing you make during your jumping session. It is the frequency of jumping that poses your greatest threat of injury in jump rope training. If you use proper technique and jump on a surface that both absorbs impact and offers rebound properties, you reduce your risk of injury and enable yourself to derive the greatest training benefits from your rope-jumping program.

Regardless of which technique you are using, you must land softly on the balls of your feet. It is during the landing phase that you develop balance while subtle neuromuscular adjustments prepare your body for the subsequent load and flight phases (see figure 3.3).

Your landing should be soft and silent, forcing you to concentrate on perfect balance and on delicately positioning your feet during each jump. Your heels should not touch. If your heels hit the floor, or if your feet land with an emphatic slap, you are using an improper technique and thus reducing your training benefits and increasing your risk of injury. Intense concentration helps you keep your contact with the jumping surface as short as possible, which reduces stress in your hips, knees, and ankles.

When you do successive jumps, you draw on muscle groups throughout your body to reestablish balance and propulsion during each jump. In this respect, rope jumping is similar to resistance training, which requires subtle adjustments in several muscle groups in order to balance the weight as you lift and lower it. In many ways, rope jumping is also similar to running. If you fail to run with proper form, you risk fatigue and injury. Proper form allows you to maximize the benefits of the exercise and reduce your risk of injury. If you manage the multiple movements required for proper rope-jumping form, you not only enjoy aerobic and anaerobic training effects but also develop the kinesthetic sense that enhances your balance, rhythm, and timing while producing graceful movement.

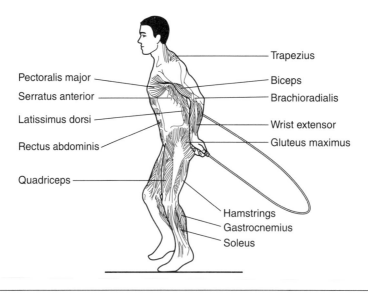

Figure 3.3 Muscles used during the landing phase.

Body Position

In addition to reinforcing your ability to take a position of readiness, rope jumping improves your posture. Stand upright with your head positioned squarely above your shoulders and your eyes focused straight ahead. Your knees should be slightly bent, and your feet should be placed no farther than shoulder-width apart. Your body weight should be gently balanced on the balls of your feet (see figure 3.4). This is a natural position to assume before performing any type of standing jump.

You may be able to run or walk with your back tilted forward or backward, but neither of these postures provides the balance necessary for you to make a series of successive jumps. In fact, taking such an unbalanced starting position can cause you to waste energy as you work to reestablish the balance required to make successive jumps. An unbalanced starting position also increases your potential for injury.

An upright, balanced posture, in contrast, allows you to execute jumping movements without wasting energy or causing excessive stress in your muscles and joints. Thus, proper body position is crucial to jumping rope for extended periods of continuation. Your arms should be in a natural, relaxed position and loosely extended so that your hands can be located on a horizontal plane extending out from your hips. This hand position allows you to jump with precision

Figure 3.4 Starting position for jumping.

for significant periods of time; it also reinforces balance and your natural center of gravity. Some competitive jumpers, who may shorten the rope length to force them to jump at extremely high-intensity levels, may position their hands on a horizontal plane extending from a position about 2 to 3 inches (about 5 to 7.5 cm) below their hips. However, there is no need for you to use such hand positions when using my jump rope training programs; these positions may improve your speed but may also make it very difficult for you to execute crossover jumps and other techniques.

Proper Grip

Be sure to use a rope with a handle that you can grip comfortably without holding it tightly in your hand. A tight grip forces you to exert too much energy by using excessive movement to turn the rope; it can also cause muscle strains in the hand, wrist, arm, and shoulder.

Hold the following points in mind while establishing the correct grip (see figure 3.5):

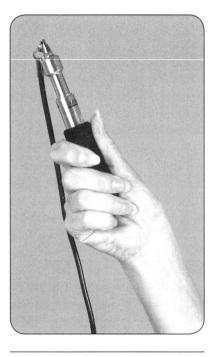

Figure 3.5 Proper rope grip.

1. Grip the handle with your thumb and index finger on the foam grip or at the center of the handle.

2. Wrap your hand around the handle.

3. Maintain a grip that is firm yet comfortable and relaxed. To avoid wrist soreness, never use a tight grip.

4. Turn the rope by making 2-inch (5 cm) circles with your wrists.

5. Keep your elbows lightly tucked to your sides without letting them make contact with your rib cage.

6. Position your hands on a horizontal plane no more than 2 inches (5 cm) lower than your hips. If you find that you must position your hands on a horizontal plane above your hips, shorten your rope. Jumping with your hands held above hip level reduces your intensity levels, or revolutions per minute (RPM), and your duration of continuation.

7. Keep the rope handles parallel with the jumping surface.

By using small, circular wrist movements to turn the rope, you develop fine motor skill in your wrists, fingers, and hands while also improving your grip strength. Using a correct grip minimizes stress in your wrists and hands and increases your jump rope proficiency. This grip allows you to hold most rope handles with control and comfort.

Shadow Jumping

Shadow jumping is a simulation of rope jumping that is performed without the rope. This practice can help you develop proper rope-jumping form by teaching you how to jump less than an inch (2.5 cm) off of the jumping surface and land lightly on the balls of your feet. It can also serve as a warm-up before you perform an actual rope-jumping set; in fact, shadow jumping for 2 to 3 minutes can serve as a sufficient warm-up or cool-down activity for jump rope training, resistance training, and other sports training regimens. Shadow jumping can also be conducted for 1 minute between sets during resistance or weight training.

Shadow jumping consists of three phases.

1. Simulate the takeoff and landing phases of rope jumping without the rope. Jump in place (no more than 3/4 inch [1.9 cm] off the surface) while making small circular movements with your wrists. Perform 25 jumps.

2. Swing the rope to the side of your body in time and rhythm with each jump (see figure 3.6). Perform 25 jumps.

3. Rest the rope behind your calves with your knees slightly bent (see figure 3.7). Grip the handles and hold your hands parallel with the jumping surface while extending your hands forward. Keep your arms close to your sides while swinging the rope back at waist level and making one quick circular wrist movement the size of a dinner plate in order to create enough centrifugal force to pull the rope over your head and around your body. Afterward, the rope should rest in front of your feet. Practice swinging the rope in an even arc over your body (see figure 3.8). The loop should be wide enough for you to easily jump through. Do this 25 times without actually jumping over the rope. This is the initial rope swing. As described later in the chapter, when you are learning to jump continuously, you should execute each rope swing by following the initial rope swing with quick wrist movements the size of a quarter.

> *U*se shadow jumping as an opportunity to become aware of how multiple muscle groups are used to sustain the rhythm of the jumping reflex.
>
> TIP

Figure 3.6 Swinging the rope to the side of the body in shadow jumping.

Figure 3.7 Resting the rope behind the knees.

Figure 3.8 Swinging the rope in an even arc over the body.

If you're jumping properly, you'll feel a continuous natural jumping reflex from your ankles up through your calves, quadriceps, hamstrings, and gluteus muscles. The feel for this reflex is generated by numerous muscle contractions and stretches and is unique for each person. You must become aware of how this movement feels for you and how it is generated by your own body; for some, it is generated by a slight contraction of the ankles. As your awareness increases, you'll notice that the jumping movement can be triggered by an abdominal contraction that can be regulated by your breathing. This contraction may feel like a burst of energy.

Some people report a burst of energy that feels like a natural springing movement starting

Jump Safety Tips

In order to eliminate excessive upper- and lower-body movements that can cause injury, you should maintain correct body posture and positioning throughout all of my jump rope techniques and training programs. Here's how:

- Keep your head positioned squarely above your shoulders and focus straight ahead.
- Rest your arms close to your sides with your elbows bent at a 45-degree angle.
- Position your hands at waist level with the rope handles parallel to the jumping surface.
- Make small circular movements with your wrists.
- Jump only high enough to clear the rope (1/2 to 3/4 inch [1.3 to 1.9 cm] off the surface).
- Land lightly on the balls of your feet.

from the balls of their feet, sustained by their ankles, and reinforced by muscle contractions in their quadriceps, hamstrings, and glutes. As you develop your rope-jumping skills, you'll begin to feel how each jump is generated and sustained by the coordinated effort of your whole body. This experience will teach you why it's so important to maintain an upright posture while jumping. An upright posture allows your jumping reflex to be easily sustained and allows the force of each landing to be absorbed by your whole body.

The Two Basic Techniques

The bounce step and the alternate-foot step are two basic jump rope techniques that help you develop the proficiency you need in order to improve your fitness and sports performance. These techniques also improve your overall conditioning and create the muscle memory that is required for you to master the complex movements of other jump rope techniques.

These two basic techniques reinforce proper jump rope training form: maintaining an upright posture with your head squarely above your shoulders and your eyes facing ahead (which helps you maintain balance); beginning your jump when the rope reaches the top of your head; and becoming aware of the stretch–shortening cycle that is a critical part of each jump.

The bounce and alternate-foot step also serve as the best techniques for establishing your training baselines and testing your conditioning and proficiency.

THE BOUNCE STEP

The bounce step is simple and effective. To perform it, you repeatedly jump off of both feet while maintaining a jump height that just clears the rope. You should time the swing of the rope while jumping with both feet.

BENEFITS

- Improves quickness, balance, and the lightness of foot necessary for agile and omnidirectional movements.

PROCEDURE

1. Jump with your feet together.
2. Jump just high enough to clear the rope (no more than 3/4 inch [1.9 cm] from the jumping surface) by pushing from the balls of your feet while slightly bending your knees and flexing your ankles.
3. Land lightly on the balls of your feet.
4. Stay on the balls of your feet and repeat steps 2 and 3.

TECHNIQUE TIPS

- Bounce only once per swing of the rope—don't double-bounce.
- Begin with one jump at a time to establish timing and rhythm, then increase to 5 jumps per set.
- Master the bounce step before attempting the alternate-foot step.

ALTERNATE-FOOT STEP

This movement is similar to the bounce step. Instead of jumping with two feet, however, alternate jumping with one foot at a time, as if you were running in place.

BENEFITS

- Helps you develop a quick first step, the ability to efficiently change direction, and improves your start speed.

PROCEDURE

1. Jump by lifting your knees forward *without kicking your feet backward* (kicking your feet behind you while executing this technique can cause your feet to catch the rope). You may raise your nonjumping foot a little higher than an inch (2.5 cm) from the jumping surface.
2. Swing the rope around and jump over it with one foot; on the second turn of the rope, jump over it with your other foot.
3. Continue alternating your feet (lifting your knees as if you were jogging in place) at a slow pace until you establish a comfortable jumping rhythm.
4. Count only the jumps with your right foot, then multiply by two to calculate your total number of jumps per set.

TECHNIQUE TIPS

- After jumping with one foot, be sure to wait for the rope to pass over your head before you initiate the next jump.
- Bounce quickly and gently on the balls of your feet. Do not double-bounce. Do not kick your feet backward.

technique

Base Program 1:
Developing Jump Rope Proficiency

Rope jumping is a skilled movement that takes discipline and practice to master. Thus, if you are an athlete, the best time to master this skilled movement is during your sport's off-season. In any case, take the time to develop basic jump rope proficiency—the ability to execute 140 or more consecutive jumps with both the basic and the alternate-foot step techniques and with no catches or tangles of the rope. It is important that you develop the ability to perform this level of continuation before moving on to base program 2. Here are the steps for completing program 1:

1. Practice to master the two basic skills of jumping; master the bounce step first, then move on to the alternate-foot step.
2. Your goal is to execute 1 set of 140 jumps without a miss in 5 sessions per week.
3. Begin with as few as 5 to 10 jumps per set. Do a total of 10 sets per training session. Jump for 5 minutes. Rest as needed between sets.
4. Gradually increase your number of jumps in each set by adding 10 to 25 reps in subsequent sessions as your timing and jump rope capacity improve. As your proficiency improves, you will need fewer sets to reach 140 consecutive jumps in each session.
5. Follow the same steps for mastering the alternate-foot step.

Don't worry about speed or endurance at this time. For now, it is important for you to practice coordinating the rope swing with each jump. As your body develops muscle memory and your brain makes the proper neural connections, you will enjoy dramatic improvement in your timing, rhythm, speed, and endurance.

In the meantime, be prepared for numerous catches and tangles of the rope. As your proficiency improves, so will your conditioning; in turn, as your conditioning improves, catches and tangles of the rope will be reduced to occasional inconveniences.

Initially, rope jumping can be a frustrating experience. This is part of learning a new skill. With practice, you'll discover your own unique style and rhythm of jumping. You'll learn how best to make subtle adjustments in posture, body position, and effort that will lead you to increased proficiency and fitness. Therefore, as you learn this new skilled movement, remember to do the following:

- Be patient with yourself—it takes time to learn a new skill.
- Stay committed to practicing. Never give up.
- Practice jumping as a warm-up before engaging in sports activities.
- Use visualization to mentally simulate improvements in conditioning and proficiency.
- Jump in front of a mirror to learn correct form.

Once you are able to make at least 140 consecutive jumps with the bounce step and the alternate-foot step—probably in 1 to 2 weeks—you have developed the basic jump rope *proficiency* and *skill* that you need in order to begin learning the 15 basic jump rope training techniques described in chapter 4. However, the jump rope training programs presented in this book will not provide you with the training benefits you seek until you also develop basic jump rope *capacity* by completing the 3-step conditioning program described in the remainder of this chapter and in chapters 4 and 5.

Base Program 2: Developing Jump Rope Capacity

Jump rope proficiency and jump rope capacity are two different things. Proficiency is a basic skill level that is generally unrelated to the levels of fitness that are associated with jump rope capacity. Jump rope *proficiency* is a measure of how well you jump—your jump rope skill level. Jump rope *capacity*, on the other hand, is a measure of your ability to jump rope at various intensity levels at a reasonable level of proficiency. Therefore, your jump rope capacity is dependent upon your jump rope proficiency. In addition, as your jump rope capacity increases, so will your jump rope proficiency.

When working to develop your jump rope capacity, heed the following guidelines. Athletes should emphasize proper jump rope form and gradually increase intensity levels while alternating between the bounce and alternate-foot step techniques. The following strategy will help you develop basic jump rope capacity:

1. Perfect the two basic skills of jumping (the bounce step and the alternate-foot step) so that you can easily make the transition between one skill and the next without losing rhythm and timing. Make 4 jumps with one skill before executing the next one. For example, execute 4 bounce steps followed by 4 alternate-foot steps

while jumping no more than 3/4 inch (1.9 cm) off the surface on each jump. By the end of the first week, you should be able to perform 200 consecutive jumps. Next, try to reach 500 total jumps in 3 sets; then aim for 500 total jumps in 2 sets.

2. I recommend that you break your goal of 500 total jumps into 2 or 3 sets. Here are three possible combinations:

$$150 + 200 + 150$$
$$200 + 300$$
$$250 + 250$$

3. Work up to 1 set of 500 consecutive jumps (without catches or tangles of the rope) while alternating between the bounce step and the alternate-foot step at a minimum pace of 160 RPM.

These gradual increases in exercise intensity will enable you to improve both your cardiovascular conditioning and your coordination of the multijoint muscle groups necessary to execute more difficult jump rope techniques. When you increase exercise intensity, you prepare your body for the energy system demands and proficiency levels necessary for training in the conditioning phase.

The ultimate goal of this phase is to reach 500 jumps per session, in 4 or 5 sessions per week, for a period of 2 weeks.

Step 2: Conditioning Phase— Develop Jump Skills and Endurance

The purpose of chapters 2 and 3 was to help you prepare by obtaining the proper equipment and developing the basic jump rope proficiency and capacity you need in order to take the next step in my jump rope training system. Improper preparation can leave you prone to using poor technique, which can reduce your training benefits and increase your risk of injury. Thus the base phase introduced you to basic rope-jumping skills that provide the foundation for conditioning and sports training.

You do not need to meet high performance standards while learning the 26 jump rope training techniques outlined in this chapter. You do, however, need to develop sufficient jump rope proficiency to execute combinations of rope-jumping techniques. Therefore, it is important for you to concentrate on learning how to properly execute these techniques, which later will be combined uniquely in programs designed to help you improve dramatically in specific areas of sports performance.

Learning these jumps makes *great* demands upon your balance, coordination, and agility as you move horizontally (forward and backward) and laterally (side to side). The significance of agility in athletic performance has already been discussed (see chapter 1), and in this chapter the significance of agility is heightened—particularly your ability to make rapid, well-coordinated foot movements. Performing the 26 new techniques discussed in this chapter requires you to apply the same principles you learned in chapter 3: lifting your feet less than 3/4 inch (1.9 cm) from the jumping surface (or no more than a few inches during power jumps), making small (1 in) circular motions with your wrists in order to turn the rope, landing lightly on the balls of your feet, and executing all other aspects of proper form.

The 26 techniques presented here presuppose that you have mastered the two basic jump rope skills—the bounce step and the alternate-foot step. Athletes who struggle when learning new skills should use the shadow jumping tips discussed in chapter 3. Here is an overview of shadow jumping: Practice each skill (jumping technique) by executing the movements without the rope while imagining that you are holding the rope in your hands. When possible, practice each skill with a rope by holding the rope to the side of your body and turning it in a way that simulates your rope-jumping rhythm. Shadow jumping helps you develop the timing to execute a new rope-jumping movement without worrying about catches or tangles of the rope.

While learning each new skill, focus on proper execution rather than on speed. I recommend that you master the 25 jump rope training techniques of conditioning levels 1 and 2 (more on this in a moment) and be able to perform multiple jumps without catches of the rope before moving on to the sports training phase discussed in chapter 5.

Benefits of the Conditioning Phase

If you increase your jump rope proficiency to 180 revolutions per minute (RPM), you will regularly activate your anaerobic energy system and prepare yourself for the multiple and extended challenges posed by the high-intensity training thresholds of the sports training phase. As noted many times in this book, the key to deriving maximum benefits from your jump rope training program is to use rope jumping to expand and extend your ability to train with quickness, speed, and power at the highest possible anaerobic intensity levels. Sufficient jump rope conditioning also ensures that you have the endurance necessary to execute the 25 rope-jumping techniques at the intensity levels that lead to significant increases in athletic performance. If you train with insufficient conditioning, you will increase your difficulty in executing these techniques and reduce the benefits you can receive from my programs.

During the conditioning phase, you can master jump rope skills at three levels. Level 1 emphasizes execution of each skill (jump) with a single rope swing at up to 180 RPM, which is enough to improve your conditioning, balance, and timing. This type of jump is called the single jump. Level 2 focuses on using the power jump (two rope swings per jump) to develop the explosiveness that is a big part of the sports training phase. Level 3 (which is optional) concentrates on the ultimate—the triple jump, in which each jump involves three swings of the rope.

The Three Levels of the Conditioning Phase

The three levels of the conditioning phrase—that is, the single, double, and triple jumps—help you increase your basic jump rope capacity from 500 jumps to 5 minutes of continuous jumping per set, then further increase it to 10 minutes of nonstop jumping while incorporating additional jump rope techniques. In order to develop this increased capacity as you learn new, complex skills, it is critical that you maintain a high level of concentration. You will also learn how to gradually increase your jump rope intensity while maintaining proper form and technique.

Here are the goals of the conditioning phase:

- Build from a basic jump rope capacity of 500 jumps to 5 minutes of nonstop jumping per set.
- Learn the following 26 jump rope techniques:
  - 15 basic techniques in conditioning program 1 (single jump)
  - 10 advanced techniques in conditioning program 2 (power jump)
  - 1 highly advanced technique in conditioning program 3 (triple jump)
- Further increase your jump rope endurance to 10 minutes per session (the criterion for completion of conditioning program 3).
- Increase your jump rope intensity level to 180 (RPM) or 3 revolutions per second (RPS).

Conditioning Phase Level 1: Basic Techniques—Low Impact (Single Jumping)

These first 15 jump rope techniques are classified as low-impact jumping, which requires that your feet rise no more than 3/4 inch (1.9 cm) from the jumping surface. To count a repetition of a jump, think of each technique as consisting of at least two movements. For example, when executing the high step, first lift your right knee, then lift your left knee. Thus one high step includes the lifting of each knee (but count only your right foot). Another example is the side straddle jump, which consists of jumping first with your feet together and then with your feet shoulder-width apart; together, these two movements constitute one side straddle.

Do 4 or 5 sessions per week (5 to 10 minutes per session) for 4 weeks. You should have developed sufficient skill and cardiovascular conditioning during the base phase to enable you now to make gradual increases in your training intensity without risking injury. You should also have noticeably improved your balance, timing, rhythm, and coordination. Having reached this point, you will find that increasing your jumping to as many as 5 sessions a week for as long as 10 minutes per session is enough to slowly build your rope-jumping conditioning and increase your proficiency. After you achieve these gains, you can add more jump rope techniques to challenge yourself and further improve your proficiency. The more techniques you learn, the greater the increases will be in your timing, agility, and quickness. This is especially important to competitive athletes looking for a competitive edge. The following gives example workouts to include in your sessions for each of the 4 weeks.

- **Week 1:** Progress from 500 jumps in 1 set to 5 to 10 minutes of continuous jumping at a pace of 160 to 180 RPM while alternating between the bounce step and the alternate-foot step.

- **Week 2:** Continue building from 5 to 10 minutes of jumping while incorporating the basic bounce and alternate-foot step, but expand your jump rope training regimen to include the high step, side straddle, forward straddle, skier's jump, and bell jump. Maintain your commitment to jump for 5 to 10 minutes per session using the two basic techniques while adding the new techniques. Try to perform 500 repetitions of the new skills during each session. Try to maintain an intensity level of 160 to 180 RPM (2.7 to 3 RPS). In order to gradually build your jump rope capacity to 500 jumps, I recommend that you break these sessions into 2 to 4 sets, with at least 1 set consisting of 150 or more continuous jumps (or up to 50 seconds at 3 RPS). Try to rest for 30 to 60 seconds between sets (taking extended recovery time reduces the training benefit for your anaerobic energy system). Ideally, add one new jump rope skill to each session during the second week and then combine all the skills in the week's final training session.

> **TIP**
>
> *If you attempt any of the 26 techniques presented here before mastering the bounce step and the alternate-foot step, you will increase your risk of injury due to improper landing, excessive movement, or undue stress in your ankles, knees, or hips.*

- **Week 3**: Expand your regimen from the basic bounce and alternate-foot step, continuing to build from 5 to a total of 10 minutes of jumping, this time by adding the half twister, full twister, X-foot cross, forward shuffle, and backward shuffle. Maintain a commitment to jump 10 minutes per session using the two basic techniques while adding the new techniques for this week. Try to perform 500 repetitions total of the new skills during each session. As with the previous week, keep your intensity level between 160 and 180 RPM, but this time establish a goal of *300* continuous jumps. During your final training session for this week, include each of the 10 new rope-jumping techniques. Again, add at least one, but not more than two, of the new techniques during each training session.

• **Week 4:** Jump to increase your jump rope capacity from 5 to 10 minutes while mixing in new skills with the two basic jumps. Enhance your repertoire by adding the heel-to-toe, backward, arm crossover, arm side swing, and side swing jump. Commit to jumping for 10 minutes per session using the two basic techniques while adding the new techniques for this week. Try to perform 500 repetitions of the new skills during each session. Maintain appropriate intensity levels and limit your recovery times to 30 to 60 seconds after each set. Also, challenge yourself to keep jumping until you reach 500 continuous jumps in a sequence that incorporates each of the 15 jump rope techniques. Again, add at least one, but not more than two, of the new techniques to each training session.

HIGH STEP

This step is the same as the alternate-foot step except you raise your knees to hip level.

BENEFITS

- Strengthens your rotator cuffs and shoulders.
- Works your abdominal muscles.
- Works your quadriceps.
- Develops your balance and explosive power for single-leg push-offs.
- Develops your gluteals and lower back muscles.
- Develops your hip rotator muscles.

PROCEDURE

1. Swing the rope around and jump over it with one foot while lifting your knee up to hip level so that your leg forms a 90-degree angle.
2. From this position, swing the rope around again and jump over it with the other foot; again, lifting your knee up to hip level.
3. Continue by alternating your feet (as if jogging in place).
4. Keep your back and head straight and stay on the balls of your feet.

TECHNIQUE TIPS

- Bring your knees to hip level (so that your leg makes a 90-degree angle).
- Keep your back straight.
- Do not kick your feet backward
- Count only your right foot and multiply by 2 for the total number of jumps.

SIDE STRADDLE

BENEFITS

- Dramatically improves your coordination and agility.
- Strengthens your inner and outer thigh muscles.
- Improves your lateral shifting capabilities.
- Improves your speed in changes of direction.
- Improves your center of gravity and stability.

PROCEDURE

1. Start with the bounce jump (feet together) so that the rope passes under both of your feet.
2. Spread your feet to shoulder-width apart while the rope passes over your head.
3. Repeat.

TECHNIQUE TIPS

- Start with the bounce step and incorporate first 1 side straddle jump, then 2, then 3 before alternating continuously.
- Do not extend your feet farther than shoulder-width apart.
- Count 1 jump or repetition when your feet come together.

FORWARD STRADDLE

- Strengthens the muscles of lower extremities, particularly your quadriceps, hamstrings, calves, ankles, and knees.
- Further improves your quickness and balance.
- Simulates sport-specific running or scampering movements.
- Reinforces forward and backward movement.
- Develops a quick first step, quick stops, and quick directional change.
- Develops the muscles of your trunk.

PROCEDURE

1. Start with the bounce-step stance.
2. On the first swing, jump by shifting your right foot forward and your left foot backward.
3. On the second swing, switch feet positions. Jump by shifting your right foot back and your left forward.
4. Repeat.

TECHNIQUE TIPS

- Shift your feet only a few inches forward and backward.
- Quickly shift one foot forward and the other backward at the same time.
- Keep your body weight balanced on the balls of your feet.
- Count 1 repetition when your right foot goes forward.

SKIER'S JUMP

BENEFITS

- Develops your timing, rhythm, and balance.
- Improves the flexibility of your legs and hips.
- Improves your bounding and lateral shifting capabilities.
- Increases your leg strength.

PROCEDURE

1. Start with the bounce-step stance.
2. On the first rope swing, keep your feet together and jump a few inches to the right.
3. On the second rope swing, keep your feet together and jump a few inches to the left.
4. Repeat.

TECHNIQUE TIPS

- Move your feet only a few inches to each side.
- Keep your feet together and your torso upright.
- Your movement should resemble a skier's slalom.
- Count 1 repetition when your feet land back to the right.

BELL JUMP

- Develops your coordination, balance, and agility.
- Strengthens your quadriceps and knees.
- Builds your explosiveness.
- Improves your proprioception in your ankles.
- Improves your lateral and horizontal shifting capabilities.

PROCEDURE

1. Start with the bounce-step stance.
2. On the first swing, keep your feet together and jump a few inches forward.
3. On the second swing, keep your feet together and jump a few inches backward.
4. Repeat.

TECHNIQUE TIPS

- Move your feet only a few inches back and forth.
- Keep your feet together.
- Your movements should resemble the action of a bell clapper.
- Count 1 repetition when your feet land a few inches back.

HALF TWISTER

This technique prepares you to learn the full twister.

BENEFITS

- Develops muscle strength in your hips and improves trunk rotation and flexibility.
- Improves your shifting and dodging abilities.

PROCEDURE

1. Start with the bounce-step stance.
2. On the first swing, bounce-jump and twist the lower half of your body so that your feet land with your toes pointed to the right.
3. On the second swing, bounce-jump and face forward by returning to the starting position.
4. On the third swing, bounce-jump and twist the lower half of your body so that your feet land with your toes pointed to the left.
5. Repeat this 3-swing sequence.

TECHNIQUE TIPS

- Twist only the lower half of your body.
- Keep your arms, hands, and wrists in correct jump rope posture where they are relaxed and close to the body during the entire movement.
- Keep your torso upright and your head facing forward.
- Count 1 repetition when you land in the starting position.

FULL TWISTER

BENEFITS

- Improves quickness and flexibility of your hips and reinforces your ability to make rotational movements.
- Improves your shifting and dodging abilities.

PROCEDURE

1. Start with the bounce-step stance.
2. On the first swing, bounce-jump and twist the lower half of your body so that your feet land with your toes pointed to the right.
3. On the second swing, bounce-jump and twist the lower half of your body so that your feet land with your toes pointed to the left.
4. Repeat.

TECHNIQUE TIPS

- Note that this jump builds on the skill you used in the half twister; specifically, it requires you to eliminate the jump in which you land facing forward.
- On each jump, twist the lower half of your body either from left to right or from right to left.
- Count 1 repetition for each landing to the right.

X-FOOT CROSS

BENEFITS

- Dramatically improves your hand and foot coordination and agility.
- Increases proprioception in your ankles.
- Strengthens your inner and outer thigh muscles.
- Works the stabilizing muscles around your hips and groin.
- Improves your lateral shifting capabilities.
- Helps you develop a crossover step.

PROCEDURE

1. On the first swing, start with the bounce-step stance, feet together.
2. On the second swing, jump with your feet shoulder-width apart (as in the side straddle jump).
3. On the third swing, cross your right leg over your left leg before the rope passes under your feet.
4. On the fourth swing, jump back into the side straddle position.
5. On the fifth swing, cross your left leg over your right leg before the rope passes under your feet.
6. On the sixth swing uncross your leg and land back in the side straddle position.
7. Repeat.

TECHNIQUE TIPS

- Start with the bounce step and incorporate 1 X-foot cross, then 2, then 3, before alternating continuously.
- When doing the X-foot cross, do not spread your feet farther than shoulder-width apart.
- Count 1 repetition each time your feet land in the X position.

FORWARD SHUFFLE

BENEFITS

- Develops your balance, coordination, and timing.
- Strengthens your quadriceps, hamstrings, and knees and ankles.

PROCEDURE

1. Start with the bounce-step stance.
2. On the first jump, shift your right foot a few inches forward with the leg extended.
3. On the second jump, shift your right foot backward to the starting position while shifting your left foot a few inches forward with the leg extended.
4. Repeat.

TECHNIQUE TIPS

- Alternate by shifting your body weight from one foot to the other while keeping your body upright and maintaining your center of gravity.
- Land lightly on the balls of your feet. Do not land on your heels!
- Count 1 repetition when your right foot shifts forward.

BACKWARD SHUFFLE

BENEFITS

- Improves your balance, coordination, and timing.
- Improves range of motion in your knees.
- Strengthens and improves the flexibility of your quadriceps and hip flexors.
- Strengthens your hamstrings and gluteus muscles.

PROCEDURE

1. Start with the bounce-step stance.
2. On the first jump, extend your right foot back by bending the knee at a 90-degree angle.
3. On the next jump, bring your right foot to the starting position while extending your left foot back by bending the knee at a 90-degree angle.
4. Repeat

TECHNIQUE TIPS

- When your right knee is bent backward, jump with your left foot.
- When your left knee is bent backward, jump with your right foot.
- Keep your torso upright and your head squarely above your shoulders and facing forward.
- Maintain your center of gravity.
- Your movement should resemble a low backward kicking motion.
- Count 1 repetition when your right foot shifts backward.

HEEL-TO-TOE

- Warms up your Achilles tendons to prevent tendonitis.

PROCEDURE

1. Start with the bounce-step stance.
2. On the first jump, hop on your left foot and touch your right heel to the floor in front of you.
3. On the second jump, hop on your left foot again and touch your right *toe* to the floor behind your left foot.
4. Repeat on the opposite side.

TECHNIQUE TIPS

- Stay on the ball of your left foot when your right heel and toe touch. Repeat with the opposite heel and toe.
- Keep your torso upright and your head squarely above your shoulders and facing forward.
- Maintain your center of gravity.
- Count 1 repetition when each foot shifts to touch the toe.

BACKWARD JUMP

BENEFITS

- Improves your posture.
- Improves muscular endurance in your shoulders and arms.

PROCEDURE

1. Jump with your feet together.
2. Start with the rope in front of your feet and swing it, backward, over your head.
3. Start the jump when the rope passes over your head.

TECHNIQUE TIPS

- Bounce only once per swing of the rope—don't double-bounce.
- Turn the rope at waist level.
- Make small circles with your wrists.
- Pull your shoulders back when jumping.
- Count 1 repetition for each turn of the rope.

ARM CROSSOVER

Perform this technique with a long-handled rope for easier extension.

BENEFITS

- Improves your hand and foot coordination.
- Improves your timing, rhythm, and balance.
- Improves conditioning in your chest, arms, shoulders, and back.
- Improves your grip strength.

PROCEDURE

1. Start from the bounce-step stance.
2. On the first jump, swing the rope around and cross your arms at waist level while you jump over the rope.
3. After the rope has passed under your feet on the first jump, extend your arms to the sides of your body to uncross (as if you're executing the bounce step), thus creating a wide loop to jump through on the second jump.
4. Cross and uncross on subsequent jumps.
5. Once you have mastered the technique with the basic bounce step, attempt it with the alternate-foot step.

TECHNIQUE TIPS

- Practice the crossed-arm movement without jumping over the rope.
- Do not raise your arms above waist level.
- Keep the rope handles parallel to the floor.
- Do not jump over the rope until you have learned how to create an arc that is wide enough to jump through on the subsequent jump.
- Count 1 repetition for each cross.

ARM SIDE SWING

This technique prepares you for the side swing jump.

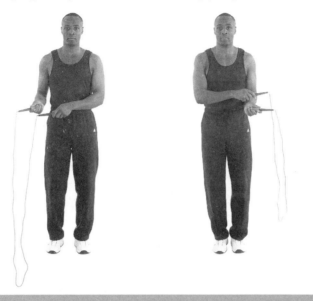

BENEFITS

- Improves your hand and foot speed and coordination.
- Improves your timing, rhythm, and balance.
- Improves conditioning in your chest, arms, shoulders, and back.
- Improves your grip strength.

PROCEDURE

1. Start by holding the rope with both hands waist high on the right side of your body.
2. On the first swing, keep your arms together and swing the rope to the left side of your body.
3. On the next swing, swing the rope to the right side of your body.
4. Repeat.

TECHNIQUE TIPS

- Keep your arms together when swinging to either side of your body.
- Move your arms only while bouncing on the balls of your feet, as in the bounce or alternate-foot step.
- Bounce in place without jumping over the rope.
- Count 1 repetition you swing the rope to your right side.

SIDE SWING JUMP

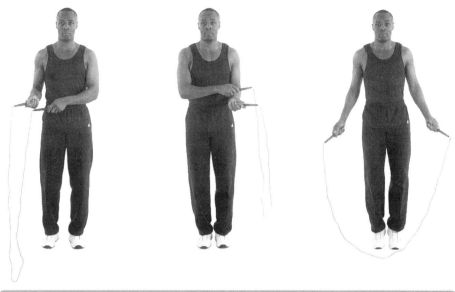

BENEFITS

- Develops your eye, hand, and foot coordination.
- Develops quickness in your hands and feet.
- Increases strength in your wrists.
- Develops your grip strength.
- Strengthens your shoulder rotators, as well as muscles in the front of your chest and the back of your shoulders.

PROCEDURE

1. Repeat steps 1, 2, and 3 for the arm side swing (see page 65).
2. On the third swing, open your arms to create a loop so that you can jump over the rope with the bounce step.
3. Repeat.

TECHNIQUE TIPS

- Remember to jump (though not over the rope) each time you swing the rope to the left or to the right.
- Execute each movement slowly until you get a feel for the unique timing and rhythm you must employ during this maneuver.
- Gradually increase your speed and intensity in subsequent training sessions.
- Count 1 repetition after each jump.

Training Tip

Establish a training rhythm that includes, say, 25 to 50 jumps per technique; then, if you have identified a high level of continuation as your training goal for the session, repeat the cycle. For example, during week 2, you might do 25 bounce steps, 25 alternate-foot steps, 25 high steps, and so on, as part of a jump rope training cycle. You can repeat that cycle until you reach your training goals for the first session in the second week. In session 2 for that week, add the side straddle to the cycle and repeat as appropriate. In session 3, add the forward straddle, and so on. This strategy ensures that you learn new techniques while committing previous techniques to muscle memory. Thus it prepares you to add and mix techniques in ways that best simulate the movement and energy system demands of your sport during the sports training phase.

Conditioning Phase Level 2: Advanced Techniques (Power Jumping)

The power jump marks the beginning of the second level in which you learn advanced jump rope skills that require more propulsion on takeoff and greater control during the landing phase of each jump. The power jump requires you to perform with proper posture and correctly use other body mechanics to ensure safe landings that minimize impact and reduce your risk of injury. It is considered an advanced technique because it requires you to jump a few inches off of the surface, make repeated explosive takeoffs, generate sufficient wrist speed, and make controlled safe landings. As a result, it takes more time to master than do the previous 15 basic jumps—and it must be mastered before you progress to the additional power jump techniques in level 2.

Adding power jumps to your regimen produces greater training benefits and all-around improvement in sports performance. Most, but not all, of the basic jump rope techniques can be safely converted into power jumps, and doing so takes you to an advanced level of rope jumping. Here, I have chosen power jumps that make it easier to safely turn the rope two or more times with each jump. Power jumps are designed to increase your explosiveness and power, but not necessarily your agility. Some rope jumpers, especially those who participate in competitions, attempt to incorporate agility jumps into their power jumping, but this is done largely for entertainment value; it is not necessary in order for you to improve your fitness or performance.

Do 4 sessions per week (10 minutes per session) for 2 weeks. Level 2 consists of 10 additional jump rope techniques that I consider to be advanced power skills. You should attempt these techniques only after you have met the proficiency and conditioning criteria for level 1. Power jumping requires a high level of proficiency because you must turn the rope two or more times per jump. Doing so requires exquisite timing and pushes your body to its anaerobic threshold in a matter of seconds. Therefore, conditioning is critical not only to executing power jumps but also to developing explosiveness, vertical acceleration, hand and wrist strength, and improved reaction time. You can combine these 10 techniques with the 15 techniques of level 1 during each training session.

• **Week 1, sessions 1 & 2:** Complete 5 minutes of jumping, incorporating the 15 techniques you learned in level 1. Then add the basic power jump and the power alternate-foot step. Practice jumping for 5 minutes with these new techniques in sets of 25 jumps with rest periods in between as needed.

• **Week 1, sessions 3 & 4:** Complete 5 minutes of jumping, incorporating the 15 techniques you learned in level 1, including the basic power jump and the power alternate-foot step techniques. Then practice for 5 minutes with the new power jumps, in this case the power high step, the power side straddle, and the power forward straddle in sets of 25 jumps with rest periods in between as needed. In addition, mix in rotating cycles of 10 to 15 jumps each for the 15 basic techniques you learned in level 1.

• **Week 2, sessions 1 & 2:** Complete 5 minutes of jumping, incorporating the 15 techniques you learned in level 1, including the five new power jumps you learned in week 1. In the next 5 minutes, add sets of 25 jumps of the power skier's jump, power bell jump, and power X-foot cross with rest periods in between as needed.

• **Week 2, sessions 3 & 4:** Complete 5 minutes of jumping, incorporating the 15 techniques you learned in level 1, including the eight new power jumps you learned in previous sessions. During the subsequent 5 minutes, add sets of 25 jumps of the power arm crossover and the power side swing with rest periods in between as needed. Mix in with rotating cycles of 10 to 15 jumps each for the 15 basic techniques you learned in level 1. Establish a goal of 300 or more continuous jumps, including all 25 jump rope techniques.

POWER JUMP

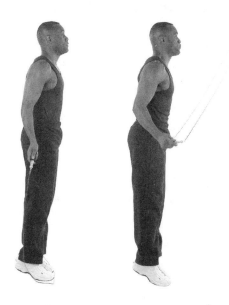

BENEFITS

- Strengthens your rotator cuffs and shoulders.
- Improves your explosiveness for vertical acceleration.
- Improves your grip strength and hand quickness.
- Increases strength in your arms, shoulders, and back.
- Strengthens your knees, ankles, and legs.
- Improves your balance, timing, and rhythm.
- Improves your anaerobic conditioning.

PROCEDURE

1. Start with the bounce-step stance.
2. Execute three bounce-step jumps.
3. On the fourth jump, bend your knees forward, push off, and jump at least 5 inches (13 cm) from the jumping surface while turning your wrists a little faster so that the rope passes under your feet twice in one jump.
4. Repeat.
5. When you have developed your rhythm and timing for this sequence, perform 2 consecutive power jumps, then 3, then 4, and so on.
6. Once you are able to perform 20 consecutive power jumps, concentrate on decreasing the height of your jump to 2 inches (5 cm) off the ground.

(continued)

7. Perform the steps in the following three phases (see discussion of shadow jumping earlier in this chapter and in chapter 3):
   - Without the rope
   - While turning the rope to the side of your body
   - While jumping with the rope

TECHNIQUE TIPS

- Keep your head straight and your torso relaxed in order to maintain balance.
- Keep your body as upright as possible when executing each jump.
- Turn your wrists with quick, small circles.
- Do not hold your breath.
- Do not squeeze the rope handles.
- Use a shoulder-level rope measurement in the beginning, then adjust to a chest-level measurement as you improve (see chapter 2 for more on rope measurements).
- Remember that the key to power jumping is not jump height but quick turning of your wrists.
- Count 1 repetition when both feet land in the starting position.

POWER ALTERNATE-FOOT STEP

BENEFITS

- Strengthens your rotator cuffs and shoulders.
- Dramatically improves your coordination and agility.
- Strengthens your inner and outer thigh muscles.
- Improves your lateral shifting capabilities.
- Improves your speed in changes of direction.
- Improves your center of gravity and stability.

PROCEDURE

1. Start by performing 3 repetitions of the regular alternate-foot step.
2. On the fourth jump, push off with greater force and perform 1 power jump on your left foot, then land lightly on the balls of your feet.
3. Perform 1 power jump on your right foot and land lightly on the balls of your feet.
4. Develop the timing and rhythm to make it continuous.
5. Repeat.

TECHNIQUE TIPS

- Start by performing 1 perfect power alternate-foot jump.
- Do not land hard on the balls of your feet and do not hesitate on the repeat movement on the opposite side.
- Count one repetition when your right foot lands, and multiply by 2 to get your total reps.

POWER HIGH STEP

BENEFITS

- Strengthens your rotator cuffs and shoulders.
- Dramatically improves your coordination and agility.
- Strengthens your inner and outer thigh muscles.
- Improves your lateral shifting capabilities.
- Improves your speed in changes of direction.
- Improves your center of gravity and stability.

PROCEDURE

1. Start by performing 3 repetitions of the alternate-foot step.
2. On the fourth rep, push off with greater force, bring your knees up to slightly below waist level, perform 1 power jump on your left foot, and land lightly on the balls of your feet.
3. Perform 1 power jump on your right foot and land lightly on the balls of your feet.
4. Develop the timing and rhythm to make it continuous.
5. Repeat.

TECHNIQUE TIPS

- Start by performing 1 perfect power alternate-foot jump.
- Do not land hard on the balls of your feet and do not hesitate on the repeat movement on the opposite side.
- Count 1 repetition when your right foot lands and multiply by 2 to get your total reps.

POWER SIDE STRADDLE

BENEFITS

- Strengthens your rotator cuffs and shoulders.
- Dramatically improves your coordination and agility.
- Strengthens your inner and outer thigh muscles.
- Improves your lateral shifting capabilities.
- Improves your speed in changes of direction.
- Improves your center of gravity and stability.

PROCEDURE

1. Start by performing 3 repetitions of the basic bounce jump.
2. On the fourth rep, perform 1 power jump and land in side straddle position with feet apart.
3. On the fifth swing, perform 1 power jump and land with feet together.
4. Perfect 1 power side straddle, then 2 power side straddles, and, as you become more proficient, develop the timing and rhythm to make it continuous.
5. Repeat.

TECHNIQUE TIPS

- Start by performing 1 perfect power side straddle, then incorporate 2 power side straddle jumps, then 3, before alternating continuously.
- Do not extend your feet farther than shoulder-width apart.
- Count 1 repetition when both feet land after each swing of the rope.

POWER FORWARD STRADDLE

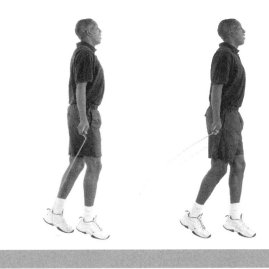

BENEFITS

- Strengthens your rotator cuffs and shoulders.
- Strengthens your quadriceps, hamstrings, ankles, and knees.
- Further improves your quickness and balance.
- Simulates sport-specific running or scampering movements.
- Reinforces your capacity for effective forward and backward movement.
- Helps you develop a quick first step, quick stops, and quick directional change.
- Develops the muscles of your trunk and lower extremities.
- Develops your calf muscles.

PROCEDURE

1. Start by performing 3 repetitions of the basic bounce jump.
2. On the fourth rep or swing, perform 1 power jump and land in forward straddle (scissor) position by shifting your right foot forward as far as 6 inches (15 cm).
3. On the next swing, perform 1 power jump and shift your right foot back to its starting position while shifting your left foot forward as far as 6 inches.
4. Repeat.

TECHNIQUE TIPS

- Shift your feet only 3 inches (7.5 cm) forward and backward.
- Quickly shift one foot forward and the other backward at the same time.
- Keep your body weight balanced on the balls of your feet.
- Count 1 repetition when your feet land in each straddle position.

POWER SKIER'S JUMP

BENEFITS

- Strengthens your rotator cuffs and shoulders.
- Develops your timing, rhythm, and balance.
- Improves flexibility in your legs and hips.
- Improves your bounding and lateral shifting capabilities.
- Increases your leg strength.

PROCEDURE

1. Start by performing 3 repetitions of the basic bounce jump.
2. On the fourth rep or swing, perform 1 power skier's jump and land, shifting the body weight to the right. To give yourself sufficient time to execute the turns, you will have to jump a couple of inches (about 5 cm) off of the surface.
3. On the second swing, keep your feet together and jump a few inches to the left.
4. Repeat.

TECHNIQUE TIPS

- Move your feet only a few inches to each side.
- Keep your feet together and your torso upright.
- Make your movement resemble a skier's slalom.
- Count 1 repetition when both feet land after each swing of the rope.

POWER BELL JUMP

BENEFITS

- Develops your coordination, balance, and agility.
- Strengthens your quadriceps and knees.
- Builds your explosiveness.
- Improves proprioception in your ankles.
- Improves your lateral and horizontal shifting capabilities.

PROCEDURE

1. This technique requires you to jump a couple of inches (about 5 cm) from the surface and execute two or more turns of the rope before you land forward and then backward.
2. Start with 3 repetitions of the basic bounce, then on the fourth rep, perform 1 power jump.
3. Jump a few inches higher and land with both feet together a few inches forward.
4. On the next swing, perform a power jump while keeping your feet together and jumping a few inches backward.
5. Repeat this movement, landing forward a few inches and then backward a few inches on successive jumps.

TECHNIQUE TIPS

- Jump as far as several inches from the surface with each jump.
- Turn your wrists quickly so that the rope clears your feet two times with each jump.
- Land up to 6 inches (15 cm) forward or backward with each successive jump.
- Your movements should resemble the action of a bell clapper.
- Count 1 repetition when both feet land after the swing of the rope.

POWER X-FOOT CROSS

BENEFITS

- Strengthens your rotator cuffs and shoulders.
- Dramatically improves your agility and hand and foot coordination.
- Increases proprioception in your ankles.
- Strengthens your inner and outer thigh muscles.
- Works the stabilizing muscles around your hips and groin.
- Improves your lateral shifting capabilities.
- Helps you develop a crossover step.

PROCEDURE

1. Start by performing 3 repetitions of the basic bounce jump.
2. On the fourth repetition or swing, perform 1 power jump and land by crossing your right foot over your left foot; spread your feet shoulder-width apart (as in the side straddle jump) while the rope passes over your head.
3. On the next take off, cross your right leg over your left leg before the rope passes twice under your feet.
4. On second rope swing, spread your feet shoulder-width apart (as in the side straddle jump) before the rope passes twice over your head.
5. Cross your left leg over your right leg before the rope passes twice under your feet.
6. Repeat.

TECHNIQUE TIPS

- Start with the bounce step and incorporate 1 X-foot cross, then 2, then 3, before alternating continuously.
- When doing the side straddle jump, do not spread your feet farther than shoulder-width apart.
- Count 1 repetition when your feet land in the X-foot position.

POWER ARM CROSSOVER

Perform this technique with a long-handled rope for easier execution and more extension.

BENEFITS

- Strengthens your rotator cuffs and shoulders.
- Dramatically improves your hand and foot coordination.
- Improves your timing, rhythm, and balance.
- Increases conditioning in your chest, arms, shoulders, and back.
- Improves your grip strength.

PROCEDURE

1. Start by performing the bounce step 3 times.
2. On the fourth jump, swing the rope around and cross both arms at waist level (right over left arm) while turning the rope twice over your head before you land.
3. After the rope has passed under your feet on the first jump, extend your arms to the sides of your body to uncross (as if you're executing the bounce step), thus creating a wide loop to jump through on the second jump.
4. Cross and uncross on subsequent jumps.
5. Once you have mastered the technique with the basic bounce step, attempt it with the alternate-foot step.

TECHNIQUE TIPS

- Practice the crossed-arm movement without jumping over the rope.
- Do not raise your arms above waist level.
- Keep the handles parallel to the floor.
- Do not jump over the rope until you have learned how to create an arc that's wide enough to jump through on the subsequent jump.
- Count 1 repetition when your arms cross over.

SIDE SWING POWER JUMP

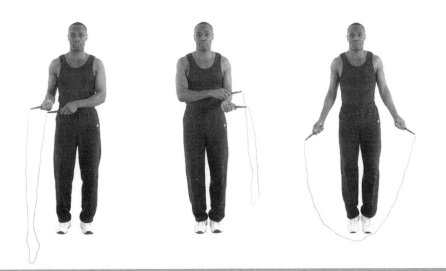

BENEFITS

- Develops your eye, hand, and foot coordination.
- Develops quickness in your hands and feet.
- Increases your wrist strength.
- Develops your grip strength.
- Works your shoulder rotators, as well as muscles in the front of your chest and the back of your shoulders.

PROCEDURE

1. On the first swing, swing the rope with both hands to the right side of your body; on the second swing, swing the rope to left side of your body.
2. On the third swing, open your arms to create a loop so that you can jump over the rope with one power jump.
3. Repeat.

TECHNIQUE TIPS

- Remember to jump each time you swing the rope to the left and to the right.
- Execute each movement slowly until you get a feel for the unique timing and rhythm required to perform these maneuvers.
- In subsequent training sessions, gradually increase your speed and intensity.
- Before each training session, take a few seconds to visualize the movements.
- Count 1 repetition when jumping over the rope and landing with both feet in the starting position.

Training Tip

- Alternate between the bounce step, the alternate-foot step, the side straddle, and other one-jump movements as a transition into and between power jump techniques.
- A set can consist of 1 minute or more of jumping while alternating between the bounce and alternate-foot steps. In addition to the combinations already discussed, you can try chunked-down combinations such as the following:

  4 side straddles, 4 forward straddles, 4 bounce steps
  4 skier's jumps, 4 bell jumps, 4 bounce steps
  4 forward shuffles, 4 backward shuffles, 4 alternate-foot steps
  4 high steps, 4 alternate-foot steps, 4 bounce steps

- Repeat this sequence and any variation including other skills as many times as possible during each session. Use the bounce step as a transition between techniques. Complete the session with 1 minute (or more) of alternating between the alternate-foot step and the bounce step.
- Gradually increase your duration of continuation at each session until you reach the goal of 5 minutes of continuous jumping. This is the best and safest way to gradually improve your conditioning and proficiency.
- You can increase continuation goals at the proper intensity level (160 to 180 RPM) by 1 minute per session or by increasing the number of jump rope repetitions per set. You should easily develop the proficiency and conditioning levels to meet these performance standards by week 3. Diligent and highly conditioned athletes may meet these marks in less than 2 weeks.

Before you attempt conditioning level 3 or any of the jump rope training programs described in the following chapters, you should be able to comfortably perform—with proper form—at least 100 consecutive basic-bounce power jumps mixed in with the various styles of power jumps.

Conditioning Phase Level 3: Optional Advanced Technique (Triple Jump)

I recommend that you attempt the triple jump only after you have mastered all of the power jumps. The triple jump represents the beginning of level 3 and requires you to exert more push upon takeoff and greater control upon landing in order to minimize impact and minimize your risk of injury. This technique is not required, but it can serve as an additional way to challenge yourself to move on to another level once you have mastered all of the 25 techniques included in levels 1 and 2.

TRIPLE JUMP

BENEFITS

- Improves your explosiveness for vertical acceleration.
- Improves your grip strength and hand quickness.
- Increases strength in your arms, shoulders, and back.
- Strengthens your knees, ankles, and legs.
- Improves your balance, timing, and rhythm.
- Improves your anaerobic conditioning.

PROCEDURE

1. Start with the bounce-step stance.
2. Execute 3 basic bounce-step jumps.
3. Starting with the fourth jump, perform consecutive double jumps twice, and on the third jump of this cycle perform 1 triple jump while jumping at least 5 inches (13 cm) from the jumping surface and turning your wrists a little faster so that the rope passes under you 3 times in 1 jump.
4. Repeat until you master 1 triple jump.
5. When you have developed the rhythm and timing for this sequence, perform 2 consecutive triple jumps, then 3, then 4, and so on.
6. Once you are able to perform 20 consecutive triple jumps, concentrate on decreasing your jump height and increasing your wrist speed.

(continued)

85

technique

7. Perform the steps in 3 phases (see discussion of shadow jumping earlier in this chapter and in chapter 3):
   - Without the rope
   - While turning the rope to the side of your body
   - While jumping with the rope

TECHNIQUE TIPS

- Keep your head straight and your torso relaxed in order to maintain balance.
- Keep your body as upright as possible when executing each jump.
- Turn your wrists with quick, small circles.
- Do not hold your breath.
- Do not squeeze the rope handles.
- Use a shoulder-level rope measurement in the beginning, then adjust to a chest-level measurement as you improve. The key to triple jumping is not the height of the jump but the quick turning of your wrists.
- Count 1 repetition each time you land.

CHAPTER

5

Step 3: Sports Training Phase— Add Anaerobic Intensity

The sports training phase is the final phase of my jump rope training system. It enables you to raise your fitness level and train in the anaerobic and $\dot{V}O_2$max zones. You will be expected to combine techniques in creative ways and execute them at high intensity levels and with sustained continuation. This phase can take your jumping skills to the highest levels of fitness, training, and proficiency. It will teach you how to maximize the benefits of your jump rope training in as little as 5 to 10 minutes per rope-jumping session. The emphasis here is on intensity, timing, and endurance.

The sports training phase is designed to increase your intensity levels to 80 to 100 percent of your maximum heart rate (MHR). These intensities prepare your cardiovascular system for advanced jump rope training programs. The intensity levels in this phase can be generated by increasing rope speeds to 3.7 to 4 (or even more) revolutions per second (RPS) for 15 to 30 seconds at several intervals during each 10-minute set of continuous jumping. This intensity level is ideal for developing speed and quickness. Your intensity level should not fall below 2.7 RPS (160 revolutions per minute [RPM]) at any time during the 10 minutes of continuous jumping.

This chapter also shows you how to use a pretest to determine your baseline jump rope intensity. You will then use your baseline as you increase your intensity and measure future improvements in proficiency and fitness. By challenging yourself to exceed your baseline in subsequent jump rope sessions, you will make measurable and sustainable improvements.

This phase emphasizes the bounce, alternate-foot, high step, and power jump techniques. However, you will be challenged to incorporate all 15 basic techniques (from conditioning level 1) into the final routines of the sports training phase. Optionally, you may also include the 10 techniques from level 2 and the 1 technique from level 3.

Jumping to Improve Anaerobic Fitness

A high anaerobic fitness level can give you a competitive advantage in two ways. First, it allows you to apply maximum effort for longer periods of time—up to 2 minutes (or even more). Second, anaerobic fitness reduces your need for recovery time, which gives you the capacity for multiple maximum efforts during competition. This capacity is especially important for track-and-field athletes who compete in multiple events and face performance schedules that reduce their opportunities for long periods of recovery. It also helps in sports such as football, where athletes must be prepared to give maximum effort in play after play, often with less than a minute of recovery time between plays. Indeed, every serious athlete seeks the competitive advantage of being able to repeatedly perform at maximum effort while requiring minimal recovery time.

To use rope jumping for peak sports performance, you need to perform jump rope training at 80 to 100 percent of your MHR. For most athletes, this intensity level translates to jumping at a rate of 180 to 240 RPM. Once you have used the first two phases of my 3-step conditioning program to develop your basic jump rope capacity, you can begin jump rope training sessions at the intensity levels necessary to improve your anaerobic conditioning. You can do this in 30- to 120-second jump rope sets at 80 to 100 percent of your MHR. If you execute properly, you can obtain the maximum benefits of jump rope training in 3 weekly sessions of 5 to 10 minutes each.

Some athletes may decide to increase their sessions to 15 or 20 minutes each because they have tailored specific techniques and increasing levels to the demands of their sport. However, there is no need for you to extend your sessions beyond 20 minutes in order to develop anaerobic conditioning. Instead, increase your intensity levels and your duration of continuation while reducing your recovery time between sets. Instead of increasing time, increase intensity levels. In other words, increase the number of RPS or RPM per set. Therefore, my training programs challenge athletes to execute as many jumps as possible in a short period of time, which should result in muscle fatigue and oxygen and glucose deprivation within seconds. For example, establishing a training routine of 5-10 minutes of continuous jumping at 4-5 RPS or 220-240+ RPMs is an intensity level that can challenge and generate benefits for even the most fit competitive athletes.

To best improve your anaerobic fitness, allow a brief recovery period after each set before you execute a subsequent set. Initially, you should rest 1 second for each second of exertion. As your anaerobic conditioning improves, you can reduce the rest period to 1 second of rest per 2 seconds of exertion. Highly conditioned athletes can rest 1 second for every 3 seconds of exertion.

Resting between sets is an application of your body's *super compensation principle*, which states that as your fitness improves you will learn to recover from anaerobic exercise bursts in shorter and shorter periods of time. You will also be able to execute subsequent sets at higher intensity levels for longer durations. This training principle explains why my jump rope programs train fast-twitch muscle fibers for the explosive and quick movements necessary in most sports. Super compensation is a process that takes place when a body part may increase in strength as a result of stress. For example, benefits of lifting weights take place because of what can be described as a super compensation principle. Meanwhile, training at high intensity levels reinforce neuromuscular processes that result in increased speed and quickness over time because of strengthened connections and growth of neurons in the brain's motor cortex. After several sets, your performance will taper off because your overall glycogen stores will be depleted. This depletion is why I recommend that you limit anaerobic conditioning sessions to 5 to 10 minutes each and combine them with 10- to 30-second sprints in the $\dot{V}O_2$max zone.

Track-and-field athletes can use jump rope training to develop fast-twitch muscle fibers for quick, explosive movement.

Although rope jumping for anaerobic conditioning demands high-intensity training, you should *never sacrifice proper form or technique* for speed! By slowly increasing both your pace and your number of repetitions, you minimize your risk of injury and discomfort. Improper form and technique, on the other hand, not only increase your risk of injury but also minimize your benefits from jump rope training and result in inefficient movements, improper balance, and poor timing. These bad habits then limit future progress.

The best way to begin using jump rope training to improve your anaerobic conditioning is to establish practice sessions where you execute rapid jumps in 30-second intervals followed by 30-second rest periods. These sessions should be limited to 5 minutes each until your anaerobic endurance has been extended to 60-second sets (separated by rest periods of equal duration). Ambitious athletes can begin working on developing this capacity during the conditioning phase of the aerobic conditioning program. Here are some ideas:

- Do 15- to 30-second sprint sets during each training session.
- Initially, establish a 1-to-1 ratio between sprint sets and rest. For example, if you jump for 30 seconds, rest for 30 seconds.
- Work to establish a 2-to-1 ratio between activity and rest period. One idea is to jump for 60 seconds, then rest for 30 seconds.

You may experience muscle fatigue in your feet and calves during any phase of jump rope training as your body adapts to the demands of this exercise. The discomfort may be experienced even in the base phase, when you are establishing your aerobic jump rope capacity. Rope jumping at higher levels of intensity and exertion may result in even more discomfort as your body adjusts to demands upon its use of muscle glucose during anaerobic training (instead of the oxygen use that characterizes aerobic exercise).

Once again, jump rope training is best used as a strategy to simulate the anaerobic intensities demanded when participating in competitive sports. Rope jumping for anaerobic conditioning is quite different from the more moderate pace of aerobic conditioning. During anaerobic bursts, your body tenses as movements are restricted and focused through contractions of fast-twitch muscle fibers in your torso, lower body, arms, forearms, and wrists. For example, the swinging of the rope can become restricted to merely turning your wrists while jumping by means of a series of reflexive contractions from your ankles, calves, and quadriceps. After several anaerobic sets, you may become aware of other fast-twitch muscle fibers activated in your hamstrings, back, and shoulders. The involvement of multiple muscle groups makes rope jumping an ideal exercise for developing your total-body anaerobic fitness. Keep this in mind as you prepare to complete the sports training phase and undertake my hyperformance jump rope training programs.

Sports Training Phase

In this phase, you perform 3 sessions per week (10 minutes per session) for 2 to 4 weeks. First, however, there is one last test to determine whether you are ready for the jump rope sports training programs. This performance standard involves 10 minutes of continuous jumping at various intensity levels while employing 15 to 25 jump rope techniques at different intervals during the 10-minute set.

You can train to meet this standard by structuring 10-minute training sessions beginning with a bounce step pace of at least 160 RPM while integrating side straddle, bell jump, or alternate-foot step movements. After a few minutes at this pace, increase your intensity level to 220 to 240 RPM (3.7–4 RPS) for 10 seconds before returning to a pace of 160 RPM. Incorporate the skier's jump and forward straddle at varying intensity levels to further increase your proficiency and conditioning. These additional movements refine your concentration at the high levels demanded by my jump rope training programs. Use this strategy until you are able to work all of the 15 basic jump rope techniques of level 1 into 1 nonstop 10-minute set at 160 to 240 RPM.

Once you have completed the sports training phase, you are ready to move on to the jump rope training programs. These programs are designed to push you to taxing anaerobic thresholds of 3.7 to 4 RPS that will pay off in the form of improved sports performance.

Athletes desiring improved aerobic fitness can extend their jump rope sets to 15 to 30 minutes, or 3 sets of 10 minutes each, with an average intensity level of 160 to 180 RPM. Athletes should maintain these duration and intensity levels in 3 or 4 rope-jumping sessions per week. These extended durations are sufficient to train athletes for the demands of endurance sports such as long-distance running.

• **Week 1, session 1.** Warm up with 3 minutes of the bounce step and the alternate-foot step at an intensity level of 160 to 240 RPM. Spend 2 minutes integrating the skier's jump and the forward straddle at the same intensity level (but trying to stay above 180 RPM). Next, spend 5 minutes adding as many as 10 more techniques of your choice into a combination regimen at intensity levels that reach the range of 3.7 to 4 RPS for 15 to 30 seconds at least three times. Try not to allow your intensity level to fall below 180 RPM at any time during this 5-minute session.

• **Week 1, session 2.** Warm up with 3 minutes of the bounce step and the alternate-foot step at an intensity level of 180 to 240 RPM. Then spend 2 minutes integrating the side straddle and X-foot cross at the same intensity level. Next, spend 5 minutes adding 5 more techniques of your own choice into a combination regimen at intensity levels that reach the range of 3.7 to 4 RPS for 30 to 45 seconds at least three times. Try not to allow your intensity level to fall below 180 RPM at any time during this 5-minute session.

Training Tips

- Be sure you are well hydrated before beginning these workouts. Low hydration levels reduce your endurance and anaerobic capacity.
- Concentrate on speed and continuation while maintaining perfect form.
- Swing the rope quickly by turning your wrists while trying to jump no more than 1/2 inch (1.25 cm) from the jumping surface.

- **Week 1, session 3.** Warm up with 3 minutes of the bounce step and the alternate-foot step at an intensity level of 180 to 240 RPM. Then spend 2 minutes integrating the bell and skier's jump at the same intensity level. Next, spend 5 minutes incorporating all 25 techniques from levels 1 and 2 into a combination regimen at intensity levels that reach the range of 3.7 to 4 RPS for 45 to 60 seconds at least three times. Try not to allow your intensity levels to fall below 180 RPM at any time during this 5-minute session.
- **Week 2, session 1.** Perform 4 minutes of continuous jumping with the 25 techniques from levels 1 and 2 at an intensity level of 160 to 240 RPM. Then do 6 minutes of continuous rope jumping at intensity levels ranging from 3 to 4 RPS (180 to 240 RPM) and including two blasts of maximum RPM for 60 to 90 seconds. At no time should you allow your RPM to drop below 180 during this last 5-minute set.
- **Week 2, session 2.** Perform 2 minutes of continuous jumping with the 25 techniques from levels 1 and 2 at an intensity level of 160 to 240 RPM. Then do 7 minutes of continuous jumping at intensity levels ranging from 3 to 4 RPS (180 to 240 RPM) and including at least two blasts of maximum RPM for 90 to 120 seconds. At no time should you allow your RPM to drop below 180 during this last 7-minute set.
- **Week 2, session 3.** Perform 2 minutes of continuous jumping with the 25 techniques from levels 1 and 2 at an intensity level of 160 to 240 RPM. Then do 8 minutes of continuous jumping with these techniques at intensity levels ranging from 3 to 4 RPS (180 to 240 RPM) and including two or more blasts of maximum RPM for 120 or more seconds. At no time should you allow your intensity level to drop below 180 RPM during each set.

Intensity Training

The purpose of the sports training phase is to teach you how to use all of the jump rope techniques at intensity levels that train and enhance your anaerobic capacity. This phase also helps you reach proficiency levels that you will rely upon in developing programs that enable you to meet the movement and energy system demands of your sport. I want these techniques to become second nature to you so that you can combine them creatively to develop the fitness and competitive edge that will help you reach your sports performance goals. Once you have completed the preceding sports training phase, you have reached the proficiency and conditioning levels necessary to establish a reliable baseline. The purpose of the baseline is to give you an objective measurement of your proficiency and conditioning. You will then be able to set training goals to meet or exceed this baseline in subsequent training sessions.

Once you have completed the sports training phase, you are ready to learn how to use rope jumping to simulate the intensity level and energy system demands of your sport. An intensity level can be defined as the percentage of maximum oxygen uptake, the number of calories burned per minute, or the training heart rate produced by 1 set of rope jumping. An intensity level can also be determined by using a performance-based measurement, and this is the approach I prefer to use. Specifically, I use revolutions per minute to indicate the intensity level for each rope-jumping set.

If you like, you can use standard heart rate measurements to get a feel for differences between intensity levels while going through the baseline or conditioning phases of my program. Heart rate measurements can help you determine whether or not your body is using fat-burning, aerobic or anaerobic systems during your training; as you progress through my system, you will learn how to determine the energy system being used by how you feel. When your fat-burning system is being used, you will find that you are able to carry on a conversation or move at a rapid yet comfortable pace. When performing aerobic activity, you will feel the need to regulate your breathing but will still be able to carry on a conversation. Your anaerobic system is being used when the intensity of your exercise makes it very difficult for you to talk. Most people are unable to maintain this intensity level for more than 30 seconds, but as you progress through my training programs you will be challenged to manage it for up to 2 minutes. As you progress through my system, you will learn how to use these and other cues to determine which energy system is being employed during your rope-jumping workout. This improved kinesthetic awareness will positively influence your fitness levels and the effectiveness of your training.

Establishing a Baseline for Measuring Jump Rope Intensity

Once you have established basic jump rope capacity and regularly jumped rope at anaerobic intensity levels, it is time to take a performance-based pretest to establish your anaerobic baseline. This pretest determines whether you have reached the conditioning levels necessary to maximize your benefits from jump rope training programs specially designed to improve sports performance. The pretest is an effective indicator of training intensity because it is a performance-based measurement that captures the *physical* and *proficiency* demands required to get the most from jump rope training. It also gives you a convenient way to measure training intensity, set visual goals, and track improvements. Visual goals could be those recorded on a pad, book, or a computer file that allow you to detect patterns of improvement in your training. A visual record will also allow you determine if your results have reached a plateau.

The pretest establishes your baseline—a critical training benchmark—based on how many jumps you can execute in a set period of time. Your goal is then to meet or exceed this benchmark during each jump rope session. The benchmark is similar to goals set by track athletes who measure their training intensity and improvement by the time it takes to run a specific distance. As an athlete's fitness and training proficiency improves, he or she sets new baselines.

When you regularly exceed your baseline, that performance can reliably be attributed to gains in conditioning, concentration, and proficiency. As with any exercise, once your cardiovascular system adapts to the demands of physical training, you may be able to meet baseline standards at lower levels of physical exertion or heart rate. Therefore, you must then increase your intensity by jumping faster and increasing your RPM in order to continue making gains in training. In other words, when you establish progressively higher performance-based baselines, you make greater gains in fitness and proficiency. Once you are satisfied with your gains, maintain your baseline throughout your jump rope training programs. Depending on your age, it can take up to a few years to achieve your maximum baseline; this fact provides easy motivation to continue improving your score.

> **TIP**
>
> *Setting a baseline teaches you that your ability to maintain proper intensity depends on a combination of conditioning, concentration, and technique. If one of these variables is off, you will fail to reach the baseline.*

Pretest for Establishing a Baseline

The pretest consists of 1 session that you can complete during the week following your first 2 weeks of the sports training phase. It is best to conduct the pretest at least 2 but no more than 4 days after the final session of the sports training phase. This rest period ensures that your body has fully recovered from the demands of the previous week's training while also reducing the likelihood of any loss in training effects; a longer recovery period may compromise your anaerobic training effects.

The pretest consists of jumping as many times as possible in 30-, 60-, 90-, or 120-second "sprints" using the alternate-foot step or power jump. The duration of these sprints depends on the length of the sets in the more advanced training programs you are entering. Table 5.1 shows an example of a 30-second pretest using the alternate-foot step; take the average of the 3 sprints to establish an initial performance baseline. Table 5.2 gives an example of a 30-second pretest using the power jump.

Table 5.1   Pretest Example 1: 30 Seconds Using Alternate-Foot Step

Time	Repetitions	Baseline score
Do three 30-second sprints.	Record your reps for each set (count right foot only and multiply by 2).	Add reps from all 3 sets, then divide by 3.
30 sec	50 jumps × 2 = 100	306 jumps ÷ 3 = 102 (baseline)
30 sec	52 jumps × 2 = 104	
30 sec	51 jumps × 2 = 102	

Table 5.2   Pretest Example 2: 30 Seconds Using Power Jump

Time	Repetitions	Baseline score
Do three 30-second sprints.	Record your reps for each set.	Add reps from all 3 sets, then divide by 3.
30 sec	40 jumps	126 jumps ÷ 3 = 42 (baseline)
30 sec	45 jumps	
30 sec	41 jumps	

Take the pretest when your body is well rested. The goal is to establish a level of performance that you will be challenged to match or exceed in subsequent rope-jumping sessions.

If you can exceed a well-established baseline on a consistent basis, you are making significant improvements in your conditioning and proficiency. Such improvements may also provide proof that you are increasing your mental toughness and competitive edge. As your body adjusts to the unique physical demands of jump rope training, you will improve your overall cardiovascular fitness and notice the following benefits:

• Improved reaction time and alertness

• Ability to exert more force while requiring less time to recover

• Subtle improvements in your overall balance and physical equilibrium

• Enhanced fine motor skill development in your fingers and hands

- Reduction or elimination of ankle injuries thanks to dramatically improved proprioception
- Improved posture and physical grace

If you pass your baseline even once, the new high mark automatically becomes your baseline for future training sessions. Each new baseline reflects your gains in proficiency and conditioning. This means that your body is using energy more efficiently while making improvements in stamina, and both of these gains can contribute to improvement in your speed and endurance. In turn, these improvements in performance may produce a justified rush of enthusiasm that fuels your commitment to your program and helps you generate further improvements.

Target Training Zones

The chart below gives an approximate idea of the target heart rate for training in the aerobic, anaerobic, and $\dot{V}O_2$max zones. Once you develop a basic jump rope capacity, perform jump rope conditioning at the high end of the training zones for maximum benefit.

Aerobic zone	Anaerobic zone	$\dot{V}O_2$max zone
70-85% of maximum heart rate (MHR)	85-95% of MHR	95-100% of MHR

Finding Your Target Heart Rate

To quickly determine your target heart rate or training zone, jump for 1 minute at a high speed, then stop and take your pulse for 10 seconds (at your wrist, neck, or temple). Multiply the result by 6 to get the rate in beats per minute. In order to *calculate* your target heart rates, you must find your maximum heart rate. There are several ways to calculate your MHR, and most of them are inexact (it takes a cardiologist to determine your precise MHR). In addition, MHR can be influenced by factors other than training and fitness—for example, genetic factors. Nevertheless, a standard formula can give you a reasonable approximation of your MHR: 220 – your age. Keep in mind that this figure may be off by 10 beats—and that better-conditioned athletes may be able to sustain training intensities at the MHR of people who are 5 or 10 years their junior.

Once you have established your MHR, you can use the following formula to calculate your target heart rate (HR):

70 percent of MHR = target HR for aerobic training zone (low end)

95 percent of MHR = target HR for anaerobic training zone (high end)

The following chart shows an example of a 40-year-old male who used 220 – his age to determine his MHR.

Example for a 40-year old

Maximum heart rate (MHR)	Aerobic training zone (70-85% of MHR)	Anaerobic training zone (85-95% of MHR)	$\dot{V}O_2$max training redline zone (95-100% of MHR)
180 (220 – 40 = 180)	126-153	153-171	171-180

Performance-Based (RPM and RPS) Chart

Rope jumping can range from speeds of 140 RPM (2.3 revolutions per second [RPS]) at the low end of the aerobic training zone to more than 240 RPM (4 RPS) at $\dot{V}O_2$max. As you become better conditioned, you can reach for higher anaerobic thresholds to make meaningful gains in training and fitness.

As you develop your rope-jumping skill, you will expend less energy while jumping at high-intensity levels. This improvement results from your body's ability to adapt to training routines. If you notice such an effect, here are a few things you can do to continue making training and fitness gains:

- Vary your rope speed during each set and throughout each training session.
- Incorporate a variety of upper-body and lower-body movements and techniques.
- Use all planes of the jumping surface while executing forward, backward, and lateral motions.

Though it is difficult to equate RPM or RPS with training heart rate, tables 5.3 and 5.4 can be used as guidelines. Keep in mind that it probably

Jump Rope Training for a National Strength and Conditioning Coach

Malcom Pugh is a national strength and conditioning specialist and a long-time ambassador of jump rope training in Wales. He has promoted my system and integrated my high-intensity jump rope programs into training world class amateur and professional athletes. These athletes compete in various sports, which include rugby, soccer, and martial arts.

These athletes claimed to receive numerous benefits from my jump rope training program. These benefits include increases in speed, agility, endurance, and reaction times. They also reported that jumping rope at high intensity levels helped them maintain fierce levels of competitiveness during sports events.

Table 5.3   Intensity Chart Using the Alternate-Foot Step

RPS	RPM (right foot × 2)	Fitness level	Approximate target heart rate (% of MHR)	Suggested rope measurement
2.0-2.3	120-140	Warm-up	60-70	Underarm
2.3-2.7	140-160	Aerobic (low)	70-75	Underarm
2.7-3.0	160-180	Aerobic (high)	75-80	Underarm
3.0-3.3	180-200	Anaerobic (low)	80-85	Upper chest
3.3-3.7	200-220	Anaerobic (high)	85-90	Upper chest
3.7-4+	220-240+	$\dot{V}O_2$max (very high)	90-100	Lower chest

Table 5.4   Intensity Chart Using the Power Jump

RPS	RPM	Fitness level	Approximate target heart rate (% of MHR)	Suggested rope measurement
1.0-1.2	60-70	Aerobic (low)	70-75	Underarm
1.2-1.3	70-80	Aerobic (high)	75-80	Underarm
1.3-1.7	80-100	Anaerobic (low)	80-85	Upper chest
1.7-2.0	100-120	Anaerobic (high)	85-90	Upper chest
2.0+	120+	$\dot{V}O_2$max (very high)	90-100	Lower chest

is best to rely on performance-based measurements (by using the pretest) to determine increases in your overall anaerobic conditioning, speed, quickness, and agility as you work through my training programs.

Now that you have completed all three phases of my conditioning system, you should have mastered all of the techniques and developed a 10-minute jump rope capacity with high-intensity intervals peaking in the range of 3.7 to 4 RPS and without sacrificing your form.

Completing the sports training phase is essential to preparing your mind and body for my jump rope programs presented in part II of this book. It takes a while to develop this jump rope conditioning foundation, but it is the key to maximizing the benefits you derive from my programs.

In the following chapters, you will work on further developing your anaerobic capacity, since my programs target the high end of the anaerobic system (the $\dot{V}O_2$max), thus pushing your fitness level through the roof. Only when you have reached this level can you expect to begin receiving the incredible results that translate into championship performance.

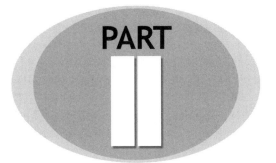

JUMP ROPE
TRAINING PROGRAMS

CHAPTER

6

Build Endurance

Today, the importance of aerobic conditioning in sports performance extends to competitions that in the past were considered leisure activities. Professional golfers and bowlers have discovered the benefits of aerobic fitness, even though their sports do not demand the same levels of physical exertion required of, say, basketball or soccer players. Aerobic conditioning is defined as how effectively your body uses oxygen to generate energy for long-term athletic performance. *Anaerobic* conditioning, on the other hand, is necessary for explosive athletic movements.

An aerobically conditioned athlete can fare much better than a less-conditioned one in activities such as golf. An *anaerobically* fit athlete can channel latent explosiveness into activities and movements that seem to unfold at a slow pace. For example, certain points in a golfer's swing demand both power and explosiveness. Similarly, whereas a bowler's approach may be relaxed, the release often involves a subtle explosive movement generated by the wrist and hand. Thus, even though a competitive golfer or bowler does not race up and down a court or field, his or her sport does involve movements and physical stresses that require mental discipline and fine motor skills. Both sports, at the competitive level, also require physical endurance. A round of golf, for example, may take several hours and require 4 or more miles of walking. In some competitions, a bowler may be required to bowl 50 games or more in the space of a week.

With all this in mind, we can see that the stress management benefits of aerobic conditioning and the intensity-building capacities of anaerobic training can provide a competitive edge in both high- and low-intensity sports. Several research studies have demonstrated that aerobically fit people experience less cardiovascular stress than do people with lower levels of aerobic fitness. In addition, once the stress response has been activated, aerobically fit people cope better and recover more quickly than do unfit people. This difference explains why aerobically conditioned athletes often manage the demands of high-level competition more effectively than do athletes with lower levels of aerobic conditioning. Aerobically fit athletes also have higher levels of heart rate variability, which is associated with the ability to recover quickly from mental and physical stress. Heart rate variability is measured by the difference between the number of times your heart beats at rest and the number of times it beats in response to stress or physical exertion. The greater the difference—that is, the greater your heart rate variability—the greater your ability to recover from physical stress.

Aerobic conditioning provides other benefits besides extended physical endurance. First, an aerobically fit person breathes more deeply than an unfit person does, which results in increased blood flow and oxygenation of the muscles, even at rest. Deep breathing also triggers a relaxed physiological response from the parasympathetic nervous system, and this response leads to poise, even under pressure. Activation of the parasympathetic nervous system can also enable high levels of sustained concentration. Many competitive athletes use visualization and relaxation techniques to trigger parasympathetic physiological responses so that they can perform at high levels during times of high stress. Activation of the parasympathetic nervous system during performance can also lead an athlete to experience the phenomenon described as "being in the zone."

In the conditioning phases of my jump rope training program, you develop sufficient aerobic fitness to meet the energy system demands of the advanced portions of the program. Aerobic fitness is a prerequisite for performing my anaerobic training system. Athletes who have not achieved the appropriate aerobic fitness levels will not be able to meet the anaerobic training demands of my sprint, power, and circuit programs.

Endurance Training

In his book *Slow Burn*, Stu Mittleman, one of America's top endurance athletes, offers an insightful look into the psychological and physical training demands faced by endurance athletes. Having participated in triathlons, ultramarathons, and 6-day races, Mittleman integrated these experiences with his formal education to highlight important principles that should guide training for most endurance events.

First and foremost, endurance performance relies almost exclusively upon the body's fat-burning energy system, which is likely to be activated by low to moderate levels of training and physical activity. These levels can be indicated by heart rate—generally no more than 60 percent of maximum heart rate (MHR)—and by perceived effort, which is an individual's assessment of how hard he or she is working or exercising. If you are able to comfortably maintain a normal conversation while exercising or training, then you are more likely exercising or training at an intensity level that is drawing upon your fat-burning energy system. If breathing or conversation becomes difficult (which generally occurs at about 70 percent of MHR), then you are likely to be using your aerobic energy system. As noted elsewhere in this book, high levels of exertion (85% or more of MHR) generally draw upon *anaerobic* energy systems; in that case, your breathing becomes more labored, and you are unlikely to engage in conversation.

Despite the priority of fat-burning energy systems in endurance training and competition, Mittleman notes that endurance athletes also have a critical need for high levels of aerobic and anaerobic conditioning. This

Jack Carroll/Icon SMI

Jump rope training can help develop the endurance to succeed in long events like marathons.

is an important point, because each energy system can contribute to long-term exertion due to the complementarity of the body's recovery systems. For example, glucose is the primary energy source during anaerobic physical activity, which can be extended up to 2 minutes by highly trained athletes. However, a reduction of intensity from the anaerobic level to either the aerobic or the fat-burning level allows the body to draw upon another energy system—either oxygen or fat-burning—while it replaces glycogen or glucose stores that can be used for subsequent anaerobic bursts. In addition, reducing training or exercise intensity to an aerobic level after an anaerobic burst can help the body convert lactic acid into an energy source that can further increase endurance. Meanwhile, periodic anaerobic bursts can compliment aerobic exertion in ways that also increase overall endurance.

Therefore, you can improve your endurance and stamina significantly if your training program develops your body's ability to replenish one energy system while drawing upon another. Fat-burning systems allow your body to recover from exertion at both the aerobic and the anaerobic intensity levels. Similarly, activity at aerobic and fat-burning intensity levels facilitates recovery from anaerobic training bursts. With all this in mind, endurance athletes should ideally perform jump rope training sessions that involve fat-burning, aerobic, and anaerobic energy system demands within each set.

Given that some endurance events can last for several hours (e.g., marathons), endurance athletes should perform extended rope-jumping sessions. These sessions should include several sets of extended jumping—at least 10 minutes of continuous jumping, including several 30- to 60-second anaerobic bursts (at 3–4 RPS) followed by 2 or more minutes at reduced intensity (2–3 RPS) before repeating the cycle. This cycle should be repeated until the total rope-jumping session extends to at least an hour. Extended periods of jumping at reduced-intensity levels allow your body to switch to the aerobic or fat-burning energy system while it replaces glycogen and glucose levels for your next anaerobic burst.

Using this strategy of shifting exercise and training intensity in each rope-jumping set will improve your ability to maintain high levels of performance and stamina during competitive endurance events. For advanced athletes, it may be possible to tailor your jump rope training program to mimic the sustained energy system demands of your sport.

Another strategy you can use to boost training for recovery within an endurance event is to include 1 or more jump rope training sessions per day. Performing multiple training sessions can help you simulate the physiological stress of endurance events and improve your energy recovery systems. For example, athletes who do not have time for 1-hour jump rope training sessions can divide the workout into 2 sessions of

The Story of Chess Great Bobby Fischer

Bobby Fischer, who remained controversial for various reasons right up to his death in 2008, took an unorthodox approach to preparing for the 1972 World Chess Championship. He swam, lifted weights, and ran daily in preparation for his showdown against reigning world champion Boris Spassky.

Fischer had studied Spassky on tape and realized that his prospective opponent made mistakes in competition only after becoming physically drained by the stress of the event. Fischer concluded that superior physical conditioning would give him an edge by allowing him to remain sharp and focused during the duration of the contest while his opponent's physical and mental energy waned. The strategy was successful, and Fischer became the first American to win the World Chess Championship.

It was Fischer's recognition of the mental benefits of his physical fitness program that gave him a competitive edge. You can achieve a competitive advantage in your sports by recognizing the unique training benefits of rope jumping and its potential to enhance your mental and physical performance.

30 minutes each. Note that sessions lasting less than 30 minutes are not likely to build your endurance or foster your recovery capacity at the levels required for endurance sports.

Recent studies have also found that high-intensity interval training may increase the capacity of the heart to generate higher and sustained levels of blood flow during maximum exertion. This is a different physiological capacity than $\dot{V}O_2max$, which generally refers to oxygen absorption in the blood. The increased capacity to generate high levels of blood flow appears to directly contribute to endurance and stamina. According to some experts, this capacity can be significantly increased after just 1 week of high-intensity interval training. You can use rope jumping as your personal strategy to employ high-intensity interval training in your endurance-building program and reap these exciting training results in a short time.

Endurance Programs

All endurance jump rope programs should incorporate jumping to your favorite tunes in order to help you keep a rhythmic beat and maintain motivation throughout the session. In addition, use all planes of the jumping surface (by moving forward, backward, and laterally) while executing the various techniques. During active rest, choose to jog, use a stationary bike, or do push-ups.

ENDURANCE PROGRAM LEVEL 1

Preseason and in-season

ROPE MEASUREMENT

Use the shoulder measurement in the beginning. In order to correctly measure results, wait 1 week before you consider shortening the rope length.

TECHNIQUES

Bounce step, alternate-foot step, high step, forward straddle, side straddle, skier's jump, bell jump, full twister

Training routine	1. Integrate a 30-second sprint every 2 minutes. 2. During your sprints, use only the high-step technique and strive to improve your baseline (see chapter 5).
Duration	Perform 3 sets of continuous jumping (10 minutes each, for a total of 30 minutes) with 2 minutes of active rest between sets.
Intensity	160 to 180 RPM or 2.7 to 3 RPS (75-80% of MHR)
Goal	Jump using all planes moving forward, backward, and lateral as you increase your endurance.

program

ENDURANCE PROGRAM LEVEL 2

Preseason and in-season

Use the shoulder measurement in the beginning. In order to correctly measure results, wait 1 week before you consider shortening the rope length.

Bounce step, alternate-foot step, forward straddle, side straddle, skier's jump, bell jump, full twister, basic power jump, power forward straddle, power side straddle

Training Routine	1. Integrate a 30-second sprint every 2 minutes. 2. During your sprints, use only the high-step technique and strive to improve your baseline (see chapter 5).
Duration	Perform 2 sets of continuous jumping (15 minutes each for a total of 30 minutes).
Intensity	160 to 180 RPM or 2.7 to 3 RPS (75-80% of MHR)
Goal	Jump using all planes moving forward, backward, and lateral as you increase your endurance.

program

ENDURANCE PROGRAM LEVEL 3

Preseason and in-season

Use the upper chest measurement in the beginning. In order to correctly measure results, wait 1 week before you consider shortening the rope length.

Bounce step, alternate-foot step, high step, forward straddle, side straddle, skier's jump, bell jump, full twister

Training routine	1. Integrate a 60-second sprint every 3 minutes. 2. During your sprints, use only the alternate-foot step and strive to improve your baseline (see chapter 5).
Duration	Perform 30 minutes of continuous jumping.
Intensity	160 to 180 RPM or 2.7 to 3 RPS (75-80% of MHR)
Goal	Jump using all planes moving forward, backward, and lateral as you increase your endurance.

program

ENDURANCE PROGRAM LEVEL 4

Preseason and in-season

Use the shoulder measurement in the beginning. In order to correctly measure results, wait 1 week before you consider shortening the rope length.

Bounce step, alternate-foot step, forward straddle, side straddle, skier's jump, bell jump, full twister, arm crossover

Training routine	1. Integrate a 90-second sprint every 3 minutes. 2. During your sprints, use only the alternate-foot step and strive to improve your baseline (see chapter 5).
Duration	Perform 2 sets of continuous jumping (30 minutes each, for a total of 60 minutes) with a 2- to 5-minute active rest break between the sets.
Intensity	160 to 180 RPM or 2.7 to 3 RPS (75-80% of MHR)
Goal	Jump using all planes moving forward, backward, and lateral as you increase your endurance.

ENDURANCE PROGRAM LEVEL 5

Preseason and in-season

Use the shoulder measurement in the beginning. In order to correctly measure results, wait 1 week before you consider shortening the rope length.

All 15 basic techniques

Training routine	1. Integrate a 2-minute sprint every 5 minutes. 2. During your sprints, use a three-part sequence to include the alternate-foot step followed by the high step and the power jump. Push as hard as you can.
Duration	Perform 45 minutes of continuous jumping.
Intensity	160 RPM or 2.7 RPS (75% of MHR)
Goal	Jump using all planes moving forward, backward, and lateral as you increase your endurance.

ENDURANCE PROGRAM LEVEL 6

Preseason and in-season

Use the shoulder measurement in the beginning. In order to correctly measure results, wait 1 week before you consider shortening the rope length.

All 15 basic techniques

Training routine	1. Integrate a 3-minute sprint every 6 minutes. 2. During your sprint, use only the alternate-foot step and move forward and backward. Push as hard as you can.
Duration	Perform 60 minutes of continuous jumping.
Intensity	160 RPM or 2.7 RPS (75% of MHR)
Goal	Jump using all planes moving forward, backward, and lateral as you increase your endurance.

program

CHAPTER

7

Increase Speed and Quickness

Speed and quickness of the hands and feet are two athletic capacities that contribute directly to competitive advantages in most sports. Speed and quickness are training effects of anaerobic conditioning; as a result, high levels of quickness and speed imply anaerobic conditioning. Thus, when we talk about speed and quickness in this book, you can assume we are also referring to anaerobic training effects.

Rope jumping is a training tool that enhances speed and quickness without requiring large blocks of training time or numerous sessions per week. My sprint training programs can help you dramatically increase your hand and foot quickness because of the sheer number of executions you must perform in a short time. Performing 100 jumps in 30 seconds forces you to turn your wrists in excess of 3 times per second. Your feet must move at the same frequency, and the goal is to make contact with the jump rope surface for as short a time as possible. Thus athletes who can jump 120 times or more in 30 seconds are not only turning their wrists 4 times per second but also executing 4 foot touches per second.

When you perform at hand and foot speeds of 3 to 5 executions per second for 30- to 120-second durations, you are training targeted fast-twitch muscle fibers in your upper and lower body to function at levels expected in high-level sports competitions. In other words, you will discover that the training effects of these programs allow you to operate effectively in high-speed or rapidly changing sports conditions. Also, because your feet are jumping just high enough from the surface to clear the rope, you will become "light on your feet." This term refers to the athletic ability to move quickly and gracefully and to rapidly change direction or speed without compromising your balance.

Athletes who participate in sports requiring this type of movement tend to move in a distinct way. They often scamper across the playing surface, *barely lifting their feet from the surface*, especially when they are changing direction or speed. This is why my programs demand that you lift your feet just high enough to execute proper jump rope movements; jumping in this way simulates sports movements in most competitions.

After executing any of the three levels of rope jumping over a 4- to 6-week period, most athletes should notice the following training effects:

- Dramatically strengthened wrists and forearms and noticeably improved gripping strength (especially important effects for athletes who participate in racquet sports and also beneficial for baseball and softball hitters)
- Highly developed calves and quadriceps
- Stronger shoulder and back muscles
- Improved posture and balance
- Improved foot speed due to minimal contact with the surface, proper foot placement, and pivoting movements
- Improved weight distribution while minimizing impact by minimizing contact with the jumping surface
- Improved reaction time in the hands, which translates into quicker movements for catching, pushing, blocking, punching, and throwing

Sprint training programs also demand and generate the concentration levels required in high-level sports competition. Thus, in addition to the physical training benefits, you acquire the mental discipline necessary for controlled, maximum exertion that often determines who wins and who loses.

Jumping Rope for Tennis

Billy Stearns, who coaches many of the top junior tennis players in the United States, incorporated my jump rope training system into his program and noticed significant improvement in his players in just 4 weeks. Jorg Rauthe, then women's tennis coach at Manhattanville College, observed Stearns' players and said that they "moved like cats across the court." Upon his return to New York, Coach Rauthe recommended that the school's athletic director introduce all athletes and school sports programs to my system. Coach Rauthe was already a believer in jump rope training, but he became more educated after participating in my clinic at the Tennis Teachers Conference at the U.S. Open. He now realizes that tennis players and other athletes benefit most from *sport-specific* jump rope training programs.

Preparing for the Sprint Programs

My sprint training programs are ideal for building quickness and speed. They are the first jump rope programs that use a baseline to measure improvements in proficiency and conditioning (see chapter 5). During these training programs, the intensity of your jumping will be raised and then maintained at high levels of conditioning, ranging from 85 to 95 percent (or higher) of maximum heart rate (MHR), thus targeting your anaerobic energy systems while forcing your arms and legs to work together to maximize your training effects. You should execute these programs only after you have

1. mastered basic rope-jumping skills,
2. established a jump rope capacity, and
3. established a training baseline of *at least* 100 jumps in 30 seconds or 200 jumps in 60 seconds using the alternate-foot step.

You will use the alternate-foot step during the sprint training programs. Remember to count only your right foot and then multiply by 2 to get the total count for each set. I also recommend that you reestablish your training baseline each week for the timed sprint programs. Use a 30-, 60-, 90-, or 120-second pretest to determine your weekly baseline. As your jump rope proficiency and endurance improve, so will your weekly baseline.

Tables 7.1 and 7.2 give two examples of pretests (30 seconds and 60 seconds, respectively); see chapter 5 for more information.

Use the off-season to master jump rope skills, establish a jump rope capacity, and set a training baseline. Then use the preseason to complete levels of the sprint training program that simulate the energy system demands of your sport.

Tennis requires players to be light on their feet—an attribute that you can develop through movement simulation in rope jumping.

Table 7.1   Pretest Example 1: 30 Seconds

Time	Repetitions for alternate-foot step	Baseline score
Do three 30-second sprints.	Record your reps for each set (count right foot only and multiply by 2).	Add reps from all 3 sets, then divide by 3.
30 sec	50 jumps × 2 = 100	306 jumps ÷ 3 = 102 (baseline)
30 sec	52 jumps × 2 = 104	
30 sec	51 jumps × 2 = 102	

Table 7.2   Pretest Example 2: 60 Seconds

Time	Repetitions for alternate-foot step	Baseline score
Do three 60-second sprints.	Record your reps for each set (count right foot only and multiply by 2).	Add reps from all 3 sets, then divide by 3.
60 sec	100 jumps × 2 = 200	612 jumps ÷ 3 = 204 (baseline)
60 sec	104 jumps × 2 = 208	
60 sec	102 jumps × 2 = 204	

The Three Energy Systems and Sports

Three major energy systems are used in sports performance: the creatine phosphate (ATP-PC) system, the lactic acid system, and the aerobic system.

1. The adenosine triphosphate phospho-creatine (ATP-PC) system. Also referred to as the "quick energy system," the ATP-PC system is used to perform exercises at maximal intensity. It uses energy storage compounds called phosphagens that sustain the ATP energy levels needed when exercising. The ATP-PC system is used primarily for very short durations of exertion (up to 10 seconds) but still contributes in activities lasting up to 30 seconds. This system is ideal for executing the short bursts of speed or power required in sports such as football, soccer, baseball, tennis, martial arts, and others.

2. The lactic acid system. This energy system uses glycogen, a storage form of glucose that is the energy source most often used for exercise. Well-known for generating a burning sensation in the muscles during and after intense exercise, this energy system allows athletes to maintain 2 to 3 minutes of moderate or high effort. Sports that use the lactic acid system include basketball, hockey, swimming, track, and many more. One major user of this energy system is the basketball player who needs to execute short, quick bursts and jumps followed by trips down the court.

3. The aerobic system. This energy system provides the energy you need for activities that last longer than 2 or 3 minutes. In comparison with the creatine phosphate system and the lactic acid system, it is a less rapid provider of energy and uses glucose from your muscles, liver, small intestine, and fatty acids. However, this system provides ATP for energy for several hours at low intensity. Numerous types of athletes use the aerobic system, particularly distance athletes in events such as cross country, field hockey, lacrosse, soccer, swimming, and track (see table 10.1 on page 159 for a detailed breakdown of energy systems for specific sports). In addition to providing endurance, the aerobic system helps restore ATP-PC levels required to perform many other movements that are critical to sports performance.

Quickness, timing, and power are necessary to excel in sports like volleyball. Rope training can help develop them.

Sprint Programs

Several kinds of sprint programs are presented here:

1. Basic and intermediate programs (untimed)
2. Basic, intermediate, and advanced programs (timed)

The timed programs require a highly developed aerobic capacity that allows you to maintain high levels of jump rope intensity with reduced recovery time. Don't forget to perform a specific warm-up routine before each session, as well as a cool-down after each session (for more on this, see chapter 11). These routines also reduce your risk of injury.

Perform the untimed pre-sprint conditioning programs for 2 weeks before you attempt the timed programs. Each sprint session should last between 5 and 10 minutes, which gives you plenty of time to generate anaerobic stress levels that trigger noticeable training effects.

Integrate a 24-hour rest period between sessions to allow your body to recover from the stress of high-intensity rope jumping. Because this training pushes your body to the edge of its anaerobic threshold ($\dot{V}O_2$max), your recovery strategy should match that of other high-intensity sprint training programs.

For the basic program, you should establish a 1:1 ratio between jumping and resting (e.g., jump 30 seconds and rest 30 seconds). As your anaerobic conditioning increases and your needed recovery time decreases, reduce your jumping-to-resting ratio to 2:1 (e.g., jump 30 seconds and rest 15 seconds).

The intermediate program extends your jump rope duration to 60 seconds followed by a 60-second rest period. You should do 5 sets per session and execute 3 sessions per week during the preseason. Again, allow a 24-hour rest period between sessions. Use a 60-second pretest to establish your weekly baseline.

The first advanced program extends your jump rope duration to 90 seconds per set followed by a 60-second rest period. Do 5 sets per session. Again, most athletes will notice significant training benefits by executing 3 sets per week during their preseason training. If you reduce your resting period to below 60 seconds, you will begin to place greater stress on your anaerobic energy system. This reduced resting period also approximates the timeout breaks typical of most sports. Use a 90-second pretest to establish your weekly baseline.

The second advanced program extends your jump rope duration to 120 seconds per set followed by a 60-second rest period. Do 5 sets per session. This type of program can be used by boxers and other highly conditioned athletes who rely upon sustained durations of anaerobic effort to push the envelope of their anaerobic tolerance. For most athletes, 5 sets of 120-second anaerobic bursts should be enough to generate the highest levels of anaerobic fitness. Use a 120-second pretest to establish your weekly baseline.

BASIC PRE-SPRINT CONDITIONING PROGRAM

SEASON

Off-season and preseason

ROPE MEASUREMENT

Use the underarm measurement in the beginning. In order to correctly measure results, wait 1 week before you consider shortening the rope length.

TECHNIQUE

Alternate-foot step

Training routine	1. Do 50 reps of alternate-foot step followed by 30-second rest. 2. Repeat 3 times. 3. Do 75 reps of alternate-foot step followed by 45-second rest. 4. Repeat 2 times. 5. Do 100 reps of alternate-foot step followed by 60-second rest.
Intensity	Jump at 85-90% of MHR or 200-220 RPM.
Goal	Each set should equal or exceed your baseline score.

program

INTERMEDIATE PRE-SPRINT CONDITIONING PROGRAM

SEASON

Off-season and preseason

ROPE MEASUREMENT

Use the underarm measurement in the beginning. In order to correctly measure results, wait 1 week before you consider shortening the rope length.

TECHNIQUE

Alternate-foot step

Training routine	1. Do 100 reps of alternate-foot step followed by 60-second rest. 2. Repeat 3 times. 3. Do 75 reps of alternate-foot step followed by 45-second rest. 4. Repeat 4 times. 5. Do 50 reps of alternate-foot step followed by 30-second rest. 6. Repeat 2 times.
Intensity	Jump at 85-90% of MHR or 200-220 RPM.
Goal	Each set should increase intensity.

program

BASIC SPRINT PROGRAM

SEASON

Preseason and in-season

ROPE MEASUREMENT

Use the upper chest measurement in the beginning. In order to correctly measure results, wait 1 week before you consider shortening the rope length.

TECHNIQUE

Alternate-foot step

Training routine	1. Perform alternate-foot step for 30 seconds. 2. Rest 30 seconds. 3. Repeat 5 times.
Duration	5 minutes: 2.5 minutes jump time, 2.5 minutes rest time
Intensity	Jump at 90-95% of MHR (220+ RPM) with 10-second bursts at 95+% of MHR (240 RPM).
Goal	Each set should equal or increase your baseline score and decrease your rest period between sets.

program

INTERMEDIATE SPRINT PROGRAM

Preseason and in-season

Use the upper chest measurement. In order to correctly measure results, wait 1 week before you consider shortening the rope.

Alternate-foot step

Training routine	1. Perform alternate-foot step for 60 seconds. 2. Rest 60 seconds. 3. Repeat 5 times.
Duration	10 minutes: 5 minutes jump time, 5 minutes rest time
Intensity	Jump at 90-95% of MHR (220+ RPM) with 10-second bursts at 95+% of MHR (240 RPM).
Goal	Each set should equal or increase your baseline score and decrease your rest period between sets.

program

121

ADVANCED SPRINT PROGRAM 1

Preseason and in-season

Use the lower chest measurement.

Alternate-foot step

Training routine	1. Perform alternate-foot step for 90 seconds. 2. Rest 60 seconds. 3. Repeat 5 times.
Duration	12.5 minutes: 7.5 minutes jump time, 5 minutes rest time
Intensity	Jump at 90-95% of MHR (220+ RPM) with 10-second bursts at 95+% of MHR (240 RPM).
Goal	Each set should equal or increase your baseline score and decrease your rest period between sets.

program

ADVANCED SPRINT PROGRAM 2

Preseason and in-season

Use the lower chest measurement.

Alternate-foot step

Training routine	1. Perform alternate-foot step for 120 seconds. 2. Rest 60 seconds. 3. Repeat 5 times.
Duration	15 minutes: 10 minutes jump time, 5 minutes rest time
Intensity	Jump at 90-95% of MHR (220+ RPM) with 10-second bursts at 95+% of MHR (240 RPM).
Goal	Each set should equal or increase your baseline score and decrease your rest period between sets.

program

Improving Speed and Quickness of U.S. Taekwondo Athletes

My high-intensity sprint training program has found widespread appeal in sports where quick hands, quick feet, and lightning-fast reflexes provide a competitive edge. Grand Master Han Lee, a two-time Olympian who spent many years as a head coach for U.S. taekwondo teams, made it mandatory for all of his athletes to integrate jump rope training into their daily regimen. He also makes it mandatory for his black belts to jump for 1 to 2 hours using many of my most challenging techniques, such as the arm crossover and multiple power jumps.

Grand Master Lee believes that my jump rope training system has helped his students prepare for championship-level taekwondo competitions. Taekwondo requires intricate footwork and great foot speed in order to maintain one's balance while executing explosive kicks, especially while moving or changing position or direction. Grand Master Lee said he believes my programs increase his students' bone density, which results in improved leg, knee, and foot strength generated from the ground forces involved in continuous jumping. He said my programs also help his athletes develop superior fitness, concentration, and mental toughness.

One of Grand Master Lee's top students, George Bell, who became a five-time U.S. Champion, credits my jump rope training system as the key to his development into a championship athlete and explosive kicker. Today, Master George Bell, now an 8th degree black belt, teaches the same jump rope training methods to students across the nation. Master Bell says that my jump rope training program is a prerequisite and building block for helping students learn sport-specific movements associated with taekwondo while remaining light on their feet and executing a wide variety of fluid foot movements. He believes this efficiency of movement is one of the keys to generating explosive kicks.

In fact, my system has been used to teach fighters at all levels—from recreational fitness enthusiasts to Olympic and MMA competitors—the mechanics of how to maintain balance and move deftly on the balls of their feet while generating explosive and highly effective kicks in the heat of competition.

Gain Strength and Power

Most athletic activities involve far faster movements and far higher power outputs than are developed in most strength or resistance training regimens. Thus an athlete can be exceptionally strong yet lack the ability to apply that strength at the right time and with the appropriate force to generate the well-timed explosive power that creates a competitive edge and leads to championship performance.

In completing my 3-step jump rope training system, you should have built a foundation of strength through increases in bone density, lean muscle mass, and tendon and ligament strength, along with improved cardiovascular functioning. Your tendons and ligaments hold your bones and joints in place while your muscles generate the contractions that create propulsion. These propulsions result in forward, backward, lateral, and vertical movements, and this workload can easily stress your tendons and ligaments, which frequently are sites of acute and chronic sports injuries. It is important to remember that you are only as strong as your weakest link. In this case, the stress of training and competing is likely to result in discomfort or injury in the part of your body that is most sensitive to stress. That is why it is important that you undertake full-body workouts and training and focus upon muscles or joints that are likely to give under competitive stress. The foundation of strength that you have developed by mastering rope-jumping skills and increasing your jump rope capacity has prepared you for the high-intensity training programs presented in this chapter.

My power programs are designed to increase your levels of functional strength and explosive power. The ability to move fast is generally developed through the use of light resistance at high levels of speed, intensity, and duration. Thus a lightweight speed rope provides you with an ideal training tool for developing speed. Jump rope training that emphasizes speed increases your ability to quickly develop power and explosiveness. This is another training effect of anaerobic conditioning. Therefore, when this chapter refers to explosiveness, think of it as another reason to make a commitment to anaerobic training.

Explosiveness is generated by forceful contractions of fast-twitch muscle fibers that can generate and sustain speed. Explosiveness can be described as force plus quickness. My power jump rope training programs show you how to generate and project explosiveness into critical movements for particular sports. For example, a high vertical jump has its merits, but a competitive edge normally derives from an advantage in vertical *acceleration*—how quickly you jump from a standing position or how fast you react from a position of readiness. My power jump rope programs reduce the time between the height of the jump and the subsequent takeoff phase by minimizing surface contact time. In other words, my power jump rope programs help you improve your ability to make rapid, subsequent jumps and other repetitive sports movements.

These training effects are often part of the training strategy called plyometrics. Rope jumping has often been referred to as an effective warm-up for plyometric exercises, but rope jumping itself is a low-intensity plyometric exercise producing significant training benefits that can trigger superior athletic performance. In fact, rope jumping can generate plyometric effects in a short time. This is true because, whereas you are unlikely to execute hundreds of plyometric movements in traditional plyometric programs, you may jump hundreds of times in a rope-jumping session that lasts less than 5 minutes!

Strength

Strength can be defined generally as a capacity to carry, push, or pull weight by means of the upper body, the lower body, or both muscle systems together. Strength is displayed most dramatically by powerlifters, football players, wrestlers, and gymnasts. High levels of strength allow these athletes to execute critical sports movements or techniques which would be impossible or ineffective without sufficient strength to handle the resistance of weights (in power lifting), a competitor (in football and wrestling), or one's own body (in gymnastics). Indeed, strength is necessary for achieving and maintaining a competitive edge in numerous sports, and one of the best ways to develop strength is through resistance training. Strength is generated by muscle contractions that produce a neurophysiological response, which in turn stimulates hypertrophy—the production and growth of muscle fibers.

Although my jump rope training programs do not incorporate weights or formal resistance training, I do have programs that generate the high levels and frequencies of muscle contraction that can stimulate hypertrophy of upper-body and lower-body systems, especially in the legs. These principles have been used to explain the effects of vibration training in stimulating hypertrophy and increasing bone density in men and women, including those who are elderly. More important, a group of researchers reported in the *Scandinavian Journal of Medicine and Science in Sports* that long-term vibration training may be especially beneficial for athletes in developing leg strength and bone density.

The most popular form of vibration training involves exercising or standing upon platforms that can vibrate 30 times or more per second. These vibrations generate an equal number of muscle contractions and subsequent muscle relaxations for the duration of the training session. Although the mechanism for the effectiveness of this training is still being investigated, *many researchers believe that the sheer number and force of contractions are the keys* to how this training stimulates muscle growth and improves strength. These are the principles I have incorporated into my power jump rope training programs that are designed to help you develop strength.

The best jump rope techniques for developing strength are those included in my series of power jumps. These jumps require high levels of muscle contraction and an ability to turn the rope with high levels of speed. You can also build strength by maintaining high levels of intensity—3 or more jumps per second—for 30 to 120 seconds per set during a 5- to 10-minute jumping session performed 4 or 5 times a week. This intensity stimulates muscle growth by generating high levels of contractions while also drawing upon your anaerobic energy system. In my programs, this rope-jumping strategy increases hypertrophy of fast-twitch muscle fibers, thus prompting improvement not only in strength but also in speed, power, and explosiveness. Researchers suggest that frequent muscle contractions may slowly build improvements in strength.

For some athletes, it may take a few weeks to achieve noticeable effects. However, you may be able to achieve more rapid improvement by incorporating power jumps into your rope-jumping regimen at durations of 1 to 2 minutes per set several times per session. As compared with other rope-jumping techniques, power jumps require more rapid and intense muscular contractions per repetition and draw upon your anaerobic energy systems to a higher degree. Therefore, extended durations and sessions of power jumping are likely to lead to relatively quick increases in your upper- and lower-body hypertrophy.

G-Forces Increase Bone Density

One benefit of my programs that is not incorporated into vibration training programs is the effect of g-forces upon training. Not only does rope jumping increase your muscle mass; it also increases your bone density through g-forces. As a weight-bearing exercise that loads the spine, rope jumping produces osteoblasts (bone-forming cells) that lead to increased bone density. The term *g-force* refers to gravitational resistance experienced when one moves while subject to the earth's gravitational force. Research estimates that walking generates 1 to 2 g-force(s), running or sprinting generates 2 to 3 g-forces, and rope jumping in which you jump 1/2 to 1 inch (2.5–5 cm) off of the jumping surface generates approximately 1.5 to 2 g-forces. Naturally, the higher you jump, the greater the g-forces; skiers, for example, can experience even higher levels of g-forces.

More important, g-forces produce training effects because muscle contractions are generated by your body in response to them. Because rope jumping—particularly, power jumping—generates the g-force effect, it can lead to increases in your bone and muscle strength. The cumulative effects of jumping translate into increased bone density in your legs, as well as strengthening of the muscles and ligaments that support your ankles and feet. These increases in strength also help reduce your risk of injury. Rope jumping also strengthens the ligaments and tendons that support your rotator cuff. Muscle fibers in your shoulders contract when you jump rope, thereby increasing your upper-body strength. You can use this strength to support throwing motions, which include tennis serves. These and other training effects emerge through your body's attempts to adapt to the g-forces generated by rope jumping. Research also shows that it is safer to jump rope than to jog because rope jumping results in lower levels of stress in your knees and ankles (see chapter 2 for recommendations regarding hard and soft jumping surfaces). Jumping rope on a soft surface—such as rubber, a rug, or carpet—softens the impact and better distributes g-forces throughout your body.

When you jump on a softer surface, you minimize impact and develop lower-body strength due to the more intense contractions required during the load phase of each jump. At the peak of each jump, you are actually weightless for a fraction of a second. When your feet return to the surface after each jump, your body can be subjected to about 1.5 g (i.e., a 50 percent increase in the force of gravity). These gravitational changes force your body to make adjustments, often at the cellular level, during your rope-jumping sessions. Rope jumping also stimulates the lymphatic system and can increase the flow of lymph up to 30 times the normal rate. Stimulations of the lymphatic system often result in an enhanced immune system while also generating a mild detoxification effect.

Combining rope jumping with strengthening exercises during your sport's regular season training cycles can improve your explosiveness and power in sports performance. This is true because rope jumping forces your neuromuscular system to respond quickly and forcefully to rapidly changing training or sports conditions.

Power

Plyometrics was invented by a Russian coach under the term "shock training" and was later popularized by Eastern European coaches before it took hold in the United States under the name plyometrics. It is a type of exercise training designed to produce fast, powerful movements and improve the functions of the nervous system, generally for the purpose of improving performance in sports. To understand plyometrics, think of your muscles as rubber bands. Plyometric movements—in which a muscle is loaded and then contracted in rapid sequence—use the strength, elasticity, and innervation of muscle fibers and surrounding tissues to jump higher, run faster, throw farther, or hit harder, depending on the desired training goal. Plyometrics is used to increase the speed or force of muscular contractions, often with the goal of increasing the height of a jump.

Rope jumping is considered a low-intensity plyometric activity, wherein the same principles apply but with a shorter load phase and subsequent rapid contractions that lead to more explosive hand and foot movements. The short load phase of rope jumping allows you to generate more energy for explosive movements. Longer load phases often require sustained contractions, which can leave you with less energy to execute explosive movements. In either case, power is best generated from the core, which is why total body strength, balance, and coordination are necessary to generate the greatest amount of force. Therefore, short load phases and a strong core make a good combination for generating well-timed explosive movements.

Famed martial artist Bruce Lee became legendary for his explosive kicking and striking techniques. He could deliver a 1- to 3-inch (2.5–7.5 cm) punch that could propel you backwards. His 1-inch punch was demonstrated at a competition in 1967 in Long Beach, California, where a 1-inch pad was held against a volunteer's chest. At a distance of 1 inch, Lee delivered an unnoticeable blow that sent the subject 6 feet (1.8 m) back into a chair placed behind him. This is a striking example of a short load phase followed by a rapid contraction to develop incredible power.

When jumping less than 3/4 inch (1.9 cm) off the floor, you are able to increase the number of jumps to 5 or 6 revolutions per second (RPS), which results in lightning-fast reflexes that transfer over to quicker wrist movements and shorter contact time with the jumping surface. With this enhanced speed, you are able to increase your force capacity (strength plus speed). Most athletes can greatly benefit from the additional force gained from a very rapidly delivered jumps, punches, or kicks. Jump rope plyometrics improves your explosiveness for any upper- or lower-body movement; examples include start speed and reaction time.

Plyometrics features a variety of movements intended specifically to enhance the stretch–shortening cycle that is critical for explosive movements. Plyometrics applies the principle that a flexible muscle is a strong muscle—thus the more flexible a muscle is, the stronger its contraction—and that it is the contraction of a muscle that releases its power. Plyometric exercises also focus on increasing the flexibility and contraction of muscle fibers—especially in the legs—that lead to sustained speed and explosiveness. Martial artists seem to apply this principle to a greater degree than do other sports enthusiasts. Explosive movements in martial arts seem to be directly related to the principle that flexible muscles contract with power and that this contraction leads directly to power and explosiveness. In addition to being a plyometric exercise in itself, rope jumping serves as an excellent warm-up for exercises that raise core body temperature, and it teaches your body how to safely load, take off, and land properly. Rope jumping can easily complement a conventional plyometrics training session.

Rope jumping not only emphasizes fast-twitch muscle fibers but also often draws upon the anaerobic energy system—the one most associated with quickness and speed. Because it emphasizes the stretch–shortening cycle of muscle groups in your legs and upper body hundreds or even thousands of times per session, rope jumping further develops

CURUCHET / DPPI-SIPA / Icon SMI

Martial artists need explosive power for grappling.

your speed, quickness, and explosiveness. Rope jumping—a potential low-intensity plyometric exercise in itself—also serves as a warm-up for moderate- to high-intensity plyometric exercises.

Plyometrics is designed to increase not only speed and explosiveness but also jumping ability. The principle is simple: The more a muscle is stretched, the more powerful its subsequent contraction will be. The goal of plyometrics is to shorten the interval between the stretching of a muscle and its contraction.

Plyometrics uses gravity paired with your body weight to force the stretching of a muscle while you propel yourself in the opposite direction to train the muscle to contract with power. For example, stepping or leaping from a raised surface will force your leg muscles to stretch as your knees bend to absorb the impact of the landing. You then contract your quadriceps and hamstrings in a burst of propulsion during the next leap or step forward. It is the stretching of the muscle that stores the energy for the subsequent explosive takeoff phase. This is how repeated plyometrics training builds explosive power in your legs.

The same principle is at work in jump rope training. Energy is stored in your legs during the landing phase of each jump and is released on each successive jump. Unlike most other plyometric exercises, rope jumping allows this activity to be repeated hundreds of times per session. This high number of repetitions, along with the fact that rope jumping allows you to vary your intensity levels during each rope-jumping session, means that rope jumping can also produce aerobic and anaerobic training effects. These are the principles at work in my jump rope training system.

This system's emphasis on repeated jumps also underscores a plyometrics principle that emphasizes the force production of *eccentric* (stretched) contractions over *concentric* (shortened) contractions. In jumping rope, the concentric contraction takes place during the landing phase of each jump. This landing phase then progresses into the subsequent eccentric contraction of the takeoff phase for the next jump. The gravity-assisted concentric contraction during the landing phase provides the force necessary for the explosiveness executed on each subsequent jump. By jumping less than 1 inch (2.5 cm) from the surface and landing lightly on the balls of your feet, you thoroughly train your neuromuscular system in this key principle of plyometrics.

> **T**his system further reduces the stretch-shortening cycle by emphasizing repeated and quick jumps, thus training you to reach maximum vertical and horizontal acceleration in the shortest period of time.
>
> TIP

High-speed eccentric contractions draw on fast-twitch muscle fibers while also producing more force per motor unit. A motor unit is a motor nerve cell and the muscle fibers it innervates. This neuromuscular process explains how jump rope training produces a reduced stretch–shortening cycle that allows you to derive the greatest benefits from a plyometrics program.

As you develop greater rope-jumping proficiency, the reduced gap between your eccentric and concentric contractions offers a greater potential for improved athletic performance. For example, rope jumping enhances you capacity to rapidly execute successive jumps or extended sequences of vertical acceleration while also improving your reaction time.

Power Programs

Whereas the sprint programs presented in chapter 7 used the alternate-foot step to generate quick contacts, we are now talking about power techniques requiring different foot patterns that generate the elastic stretch that trains the power response.

Numerous sports (e.g., basketball, skating, soccer, track and field, volleyball, and wrestling) require athletes to deliver bursts of energy—power and explosiveness—at decisive moments in order to execute critical movements. One way to measure power and explosiveness is through the vertical jump test. To perform it, stand in the universal athletic position (see chapter 1, page 7) and jump up as high as you can to touch a mark on a wall. Although the height of your vertical leap is largely determined by genetics, you can increase the explosive power and height of your jump through techniques such as weight training, rope jumping, and plyometric exercises. I have developed five power jump rope training programs that can help you improve your anaerobic capacity, your vertical acceleration, your grip strength, and your start speed. They also provide the following benefits:

- Increased wrist, ankle, and knee strength
- Conditioning of your back, shoulders, and chest
- Improved posture
- Increased proprioception in your feet and ankles
- Increased strength in your calves, quadriceps, and hamstrings
- Improvements in your vertical leap and lateral shifting

These programs should be executed only after you have mastered the basic rope-jumping skills and established a jump rope capacity and a training baseline of *at least* 30 power jumps in 30 seconds or 60 power jumps in 60 seconds. You should reestablish your training baseline each week. You can do so by means of 30 or 60 second pretests. As your endurance and jump rope proficiency improve, so will your baseline score. Working to continually improve one's baselines at these intensity levels (or higher) can increase your power and explosiveness in 2 to 3 weeks. In subsequent sessions at increased intensity levels, you will improve your power and explosiveness and reduce your need for long rest intervals between sets. All of this will translate into a sustained capacity to give maximum effort during your sports competitions.

Tables 8.1 and 8.2 show sample pretests for establishing your training baseline for the power programs. Use the basic power jump (2 rope revolutions per jump) for the pretest, since you will use it for all of the power training programs.

Table 8.1   Pretest Example 1: 30 Seconds

Time Sprint 3 sets.	Repetitions for the power jump Record your reps for each set.	Baseline score Add reps from all 3 sets, then divide by 3.
30 sec	40 jumps	126 jumps ÷ 3 = 42 (baseline)
30 sec	45 jumps	
30 sec	41 jumps	

Table 8.2   Pretest Example 2: 60 Seconds

Time Sprint 3 sets.	Repetitions for power jump Record your reps for each set.	Baseline score Add reps from all 3 sets, then divide by 3.
60 sec	80 jumps	252 jumps ÷ 3 = 84 (baseline)
60 sec	90 jumps	
60 sec	82 jumps	

BASIC PRECONDITIONING POWER PROGRAM

Preseason

Use the shoulder measurement in the beginning. In order to correctly measure results, wait 1 week before you consider shortening the rope length.

Alternate-foot step, power jump

Training routine	1. Do 8 reps of the alternate-foot step (count your right foot 4 times). 2. Do 4 reps of consecutive power jumps. 3. Repeat this routine for 30 seconds. 4. Rest for 30 seconds. 5. Repeat 5 times.
Duration	5 minutes: 2.5 minutes jump time, 2.5 minutes rest time
Intensity	Jump at 85-90% of MHR or 80-100 RPM.
Goals	Maintain the same speed from the alternate-foot step to the power jump. Decrease your rest period between sets.

INTERMEDIATE PRECONDITIONING POWER PROGRAM

Preseason

Use the shoulder measurement in the beginning. In order to correctly measure results, wait 1 week before you consider shortening the rope length.

Alternate-foot step, power jump

Training routine	1. Do 8 reps of the alternate-foot step. 2. Do 8 reps of consecutive power jumps. 3. Repeat this routine for 60 seconds. 4. Rest for 60 seconds. 5. Repeat 3 times.
Duration	6 minutes: 3 minutes jump time, 3 minutes rest time
Intensity	Jump at 85-90% of MHR or 80-100 RPM.
Goals	Maintain same speed from the alternate-foot step to the power jump. Decrease your rest period between sets.

program

BASIC POWER PROGRAM

Preseason and in-season

Use the underarm measurement. In order to correctly measure results, wait 1 week before you consider shortening the rope length.

Power jump

Training routine	1. Power-jump for 30 seconds. 2. Rest for 30 seconds. 3. Repeat 5 times.
Duration	5 minutes: 2.5 minutes jump time, 2.5 minutes rest time
Intensity	Jump at 85-95% of MHR or 80-120 RPM.
Goals	Move forward and backward while jumping. Decrease your rest period between sets.

program

INTERMEDIATE POWER PROGRAM

In-season

Use the underarm measurement. In order to correctly measure results, wait 1 week before you consider shortening the rope length.

Power jump

Training routine	1. Power-jump for 60 seconds. 2. Rest for 60 seconds. 3. Repeat 5 times.
Duration	10 minutes: 5 minutes jump time, 5 minutes rest time
Intensity	Jump at 85-95% of MHR or 80-120 RPM.
Goals	Move forward and backward while jumping. Decrease your rest period between sets.

program

ADVANCED POWER PROGRAM 1

In-season

Use the underarm measurement. In order to correctly measure results, wait 1 week before you consider shortening the rope length.

Power jump, power forward straddle, power side straddle

Training routine	1. Perform 2 reps of each technique. 2. Repeat this routine for 30 seconds. 3. Rest for 30 seconds. 4. Repeat 5 times.
Duration	5 minutes: 2.5 minutes jump time, 2.5 minutes rest time
Intensity	Jump at 85-95% of MHR or 80-120 RPM.
Goals	Move forward and backward while jumping. Decrease your rest period between sets.

program

138

ADVANCED POWER PROGRAM 2

In-season

Use the underarm measurement. In order to correctly measure results, wait 1 week before you consider shortening the rope length.

Power jump, power forward straddle, power side straddle, full twister, power arm crossover, power bell jump, power skier's jump, power X-foot cross

Training repetitions	1. Perform 2 reps of each technique. 2. Repeat this routine for 30 seconds. 3. Rest for 30 seconds. 4. Repeat 5 times.
Duration	5 minutes: 2.5 minutes jump time, 2.5 minutes rest time
Intensity	Jump at 85-95% of MHR or 80-120 RPM.
Goals	Decrease your rest period between sets.

program

Rope Jumping Combined With Other Strength Training Modalities

Modern athletes purposefully draw upon multiple energy systems and strategies in order to generate competitive edges in speed, power, and explosiveness. Here, I provide overviews of several training strategies that you can integrate into your jump rope training program to produce additional training effects.

Advances in sports training have coalesced into one truth that is expressed in the old saying, "All paths lead to one goal." When it comes to sports and fitness training, there is more than one route to boosting strength, endurance, and performance. Indeed, there are literally hundreds of training options, but thus far in the 21st century there seems to be an emerging focus on strategies for developing your agility, speed, endurance, and fitness by emphasizing core muscle groups, stabilizer muscles, balance, and flexibility. These strategies include:

- Suspension training
- Circuit training
- Weighted vests
- Heavy ropes

Suspension Training

This method was created by Randy Hetrick, former Navy SEAL and inventor of the TRX Suspension Trainer. He and fellow commandos used this training technique and a jump rope to keep themselves fit and combat ready. Suspension training incorporates two components that make it a viable sports and fitness training option. First, it generally relies upon body weight. Thus, unless you have a specific sports or fitness training need, you won't need to use dumbbells or other weight training equipment. You will need, in addition to your own body weight, a rubber band or other elastic material. The trick? Use the band or elastic material to stretch, suspend, or pull your own body weight.

You can attach the band to any physical structure that is strong enough to support your body weight, or you can use the bands against your own weight to provide resistance. For example, you can grab a band by both hands and stretch it while you hold a standing, sitting, or supine position. Alternatively, can also use your legs or feet to provide support while you grab one end of the band and reach above your head, to the side, or while turning your torso. You can also tie the band to a supporting structure and use its resistance to develop leg strength and balance. These lifts can simulate resistance or fitness or training movements, including kicks. The options are literally limitless, but the principle is generally the same.

Using heavy-duty nylon or elastic bands in this way emphasizes the stabilizer muscles that are required to maintain your balance while you stretch the band. Stretching the band provides resistance training, and balancing the band develops your stabilizer muscles and core strength. As many athletes and fitness enthusiasts are now aware, exercises that emphasize balance also develop core strength. These benefits not only enhance your performance and improve your fitness, they also reduce your risk of injury. A strong core (especially in the abs) relieves stress on your lower back and reduces your risk of lower back injury, including muscle spasms.

Rope jumping can supplement your suspension training sessions by adding a dynamic anaerobic component. Suspension and jump rope training both emphasize stabilizer muscles, core strength, and balance. However, jump rope training particularly targets fast-twitch muscle fibers, which can complement the slow-twitch muscle fibers generally used in most suspension training techniques. Together, then, rope jumping and suspension training can create "muscle confusion," which is an ideal training effect. Muscle confusion is a training principle that creates variety in your training by changing up the exercises to hit your muscles from different angles and by cycling or changing your training program every four weeks in order to force your muscles to grow more quickly.

I recommend that you do your own research to determine which suspension training program works best for you and that you incorporate it into your fitness or sports training program.

Rope Jumping and Circuit Training

Circuit training is another strategy that increases muscle confusion by drawing upon a variety of muscle groups at varying intensities and durations of exercise. Circuit training also can include exercises that emphasize different energy systems—all in one workout.

Circuit training programs come in numerous types. Some offer a variety of weight training stations for you to work through as you progress from one station to the next. Normally, rest periods vary from a few seconds to 2 minutes between stations, depending upon the recovery needs for each set. This approach allows for whole-body training at varying intensity levels. Circuit training can also include combinations of calisthenics, resistance, suspension, and other techniques combined in sequences that simulate sports movements or develop desired fitness outcomes. These combinations can be modified to meet each person's fitness goals.

The primary benefit of circuit training is that it provides options for versatile movements that use varying energy systems and multiple muscle groups. This versatility enables you to create the muscle confusion that has been shown to generate noticeable training gains in a relatively short period of time.

Because circuit training routines can be tailored to meet fitness or sports performance goals, rope jumping fits nicely into these routines. Rope jumping can serve as part of circuit training station or be used as an active rest interval between stations. In addition, you can use different rope-jumping techniques at different stations in your circuit training routine. For example, you might spend 5 minutes using the alternate-foot or bounce step as part of a warm-up. At a later station—perhaps one where you are attempting to develop explosiveness and speed—you might use power jump techniques. You can also use rope jumping as a cool-down activity before your postexercise stretching routine.

Weighted Vests

Weighted vests have become a popular choice among those seeking to burn calories and increase muscle mass, overall strength, and explosive power. If you use a weighted vest during a jump rope session, you will also increase the g-forces you experience, thus leading to increased bone density and muscular strength. Athletes can maximize their total work-out when using a weighted vest and rope jumping as part of their daily conditioning routines. Weighted vests are also great for firefighter and military training as it simulates the loads they have to carry on a daily basis. Wearing a weighted vest during jump rope training also reinforces good posture and can help support and strengthen your back, provided that you maintain proper balance when using it.

Heavy Ropes

Many athletes and fitness enthusiasts use heavily weighted jump ropes as part of their fitness routines. These weights may be incorporated into the handles or into the rope itself, and training with them primarily develops your upper-body strength. Some ropes weigh 10 pounds (4.5 kg) or more, but, in order to ensure safety and achieve desired training results, I suggest that you choose a heavy rope that weighs no more than 2 pounds (0.9 kg).

Turning the rope not only involves turning your wrists but also draws upon muscle groups in your shoulders, deltoids, and back. Training with heavy ropes is normally emphasized by athletes who rely heavily upon upper-body strength and endurance for success in their sport (e.g., swimming, gymnastics). However, weighted ropes are turned at slower speeds—rarely more than 120 RPM—and therefore develop slow-twitch rather than fast-twitch muscle fibers. You can generate training benefits for your fast-twitch muscle fibers by incorporating speed ropes and the techniques I have outlined in this book as part of your heavy rope training.

For example, you can rotate from a heavy rope set into one of my speed rope sets. My hyperformance sets emphasize fast-twitch muscle fibers and help you develop speed and quickness in your hands and feet. You can use heavy rope sessions, in turn, to improve your strength and endurance. By mixing both kinds of work together—ideally, in the same workout—you will increase your training effects in several ways, including the creation of muscle confusion and its associated fitness benefits.

These training options build upon current methods being used to promote high levels of fitness without sacrificing sports performance. Cross-training, circuit training, resistance training, and other options have been found to benefit athletes in a variety of sports. I encourage you to explore a variety of training and fitness options to supplement or complement your jump rope training program.

Rope jumping can also be integrated into fitness and conditioning classes. Here is a list of other popular and recognized training techniques that can easily be combined with jump rope training for a total fitness workout!

Boot camp

BOSU ball
  (a hemisphere attached to a platform to enable various exercises)

Calisthenics

Grappling

Kettlebells

Kickboxing

Mixed martial arts

Pilates

Tumbling and gymnastics

Yoga

Improving Core Strength With Rope Jumping

When I finally met with CrossFit creator Greg Glassman one and a half years ago, he told me that he felt it was a meeting long overdue. CrossFit is a core strength and conditioning organization that designs programs to elicit broad adaptive responses in order to optimize physical competence in 10 recognized fitness domains: cardiovascular and respiratory endurance, stamina, strength, flexibility, power, speed, coordination, agility, balance, and accuracy. At that time, Greg was looking for a jump rope expert and understood the need to educate himself and other CrossFitters about the importance of mastering the basic rope-jumping techniques before progressing to power jump programs. Greg felt that my jump rope training system was the perfect match, and since then I have conducted jump rope training workshops throughout the CrossFit community. During my international travels over the past couple of years, I have seen many CrossFitters—among them firefighters, military personnel, and FBI agents—using my rope tips and incorporating my jump rope techniques into their CrossFit workouts. One of them is Chris Spealler, who is recognized as the top pound-for-pound CrossFitter in the world. He is also the owner of CrossFit Park City (Utah), one of more than two thousand CrossFit gyms around the world. We all know that dynamite comes in small packages, and at 5 feet 5 inches tall and 150 pounds (68 kg) Chris is just that—pure dynamite. As a former wrestler, he believes that jump rope training has given him the explosiveness and conditioning required to sustain the high energy levels required for CrossFit training and competition.

CHAPTER

9

Improve Agility, Rhythm, Balance, and Coordination

Kinesthetic awareness is the ability to monitor body movements in three-dimensional space over a period of time. It is critical to athletic performance and injury prevention, and it is required for every physical movement—even those committed to muscle memory. Kinesthetic awareness is strongly indicated by levels of agility, rhythm, balance, and coordination. These capacities are often synergistic, which means that improvement in one naturally increases the others.

The saying that "the body becomes all eyes" describes an optimum state of kinesthetic awareness that enables one to respond rapidly to changing situations in most sports environments. This ability is especially important for athletes who must quickly adjust to the chaotic twists and turns of fast-paced sports. These adjustments include changing direction, maintaining dynamic balance, and modifying techniques to adapt to the demands of the sport. This apt metaphor refers to adept displays of agility demonstrated by gymnasts, martial artists, basketball players, football players, and wrestlers. These and other athletes are challenged to perform complex movements requiring precise integration of multiple muscle groups and deft eye–hand coordination.

Because the human body is synergistic, one of the secrets to high performance is multijoint training. For example, one research study compared the muscles and motor control systems of concert pianists, elite Olympic swimmers, and weightlifters with those of normal healthy adults. The investigators concluded that the elite performers excelled not in controlling individual muscles but in *orchestrating* the work of several muscles.

Rope jumping trains your whole body to orchestrate its movements at once, which develops the agility and coordination beneficial in all sports, especially sports with lots of coordinated movements like wrestling and gymnastics.

Agility

Rope jumping performed at high-intensity levels often requires your body to move through different planes and thus helps you improve your kinesthetic awareness. This awareness, in turn, increases your agility and your ability to make rapid changes in forward, backward, and lateral directions that can give you a competitive advantage. Agility is a competitive advantage that coaches and athletes often identify as a training priority. It is the ability to maintain dynamic balance during acceleration, deceleration, and changes of direction without compromising speed or quickness. Because sports are generally games of multidirectional movement through several planes, agility training is critical to high-level sports performance. Like speed and other attributes of raw athletic talent, agility is partially determined by genetic influences. Regardless of your genetic makeup, however, numerous training techniques can enhance your potential for agile movement. The best techniques focus upon the agility needs of your sport, especially foot movements and demands for eye–hand coordination.

Agility demonstrates proprioception at its best. The proprioceptive capacity of the body is the foundation of kinesthetic awareness and of the body's ability to move quickly and smoothly through three-dimensional space. It is up to each athlete to find ways to enhance overall kinesthetic awareness by building on his or her innate proprioception.

There's another reason that rope jumping is a powerful tool for agility training. In addition to providing a metronome-like rhythm that synchronizes the movements of multiple muscle groups, it fine-tunes *neuromuscular* integration in another very important way.

Rhythm

Rhythmic training is embedded in jump rope training, and it improves as you increase your jump rope proficiency. Rhythmics are large-muscle activities performed in time to a regular beat or rhythm, and rhythmic training is critical to coordinating the activities of large-muscle groups in graceful and efficient athletic or artistic movements. As your jump rope proficiency increases, you will be able to sustain longer periods of jumping; this capacity will translate into higher levels of muscle memory, which in turn will allow you to perform jump rope routines with less effort.

Jumping is a skilled movement that requires proper timing and coordination of the rope swing with each jump. In time, you will discover that as you practice proper rope-jumping form and technique you eventually experience a rope-jumping rhythm that builds your agility, timing, and balance.

You will find that your kinesthetic awareness, which involves increased activity in the parts of the brain that execute these jump rope movements, allows you to focus on the rhythm of jumping itself rather than on each component of each jump. This muscle memory not only translates into an enhanced sense of rhythm but also improves your balance and agility. And it is muscle memory of highly complex, multijoint movements that allows some athletes to perform at high levels in more than one sport. The key to developing coordination is to adopt a training activity that emphasizes timing—also known as rhythm.

Even though many athletes and sports reporters refer to rhythm as essential to high performance, it is rarely defined in ways that lead to a better understanding of it or how to develop it. So, here it is! Rhythm is timing. When you do something at the right time, you are in rhythm. When you do something at the wrong time, or "out of time," you are out of rhythm. If you understand rhythm as timing and recognize that rope jumping is largely based upon timing, then you see how rope jumping can develop rhythm, which is a key component of sports performance.

By using this sense of rhythm, you will discover that your ability to improve jump rope proficiency is limited only by your commitment and imagination. As your proficiency increases, so will your agility, balance, and coordination, which will lead you to further improvement in the rhythm or timing that is critical to high levels of sports performance.

Your rope-jumping rhythm can function like a metronome that synchronizes each component of your jumping in a highly coordinated, finely timed sequence of physical movements through vertical and horizontal space. As your proficiency improves, you will become more sensitive to this rhythm, and your body will develop neuromuscular capacities to transfer it from sports training to sports performance. By tuning in to this rhythm, you will also access your sense of balance, which is a critical component of agility.

Balance

In simple terms, balance can be described as the foundation from which all movements originate. It is perhaps the most important component of athleticism. At all times, your body is subjected to a force that cannot be seen by the naked eye. This force is, of course, called gravity, and your ability to control your center of gravity determines your sense of balance. *Dynamic* balance is the ability to control your center of gravity during angular and unstable body movements. It determines whether you perform with power and gracefulness or become drained and risk getting thrown to the ground. Without balance, even your strongest muscles become useless and unable to exert force on another body. Thus poor balance often results in weak skill development in terms of speed, power, and strength; it increases one's risk of injury.

As a training activity, rope jumping draws on nearly every muscle in your body. In addition to the major muscle groups already discussed, rope jumping also draws upon stabilizing muscles and muscle fibers. These are the muscle systems that contribute to your overall sense of balance. As you increase in proficiency and become able to sustain rope jumping for as long as 5 minutes at a time, you will get a feel for the stabilizer muscles, located near the joints, that complement the support of ligaments and tendons.

During sports play, athletes constantly lose their center of gravity and regain it in order to maintain balance. Rope jumping forces you to lose and regain your balance several times per second. It forces you to alternate balancing on one leg and then on the other while your upper body coordinates the rope swing with each jump. It also requires proper timing and coordination.

> *T*he rhythmic aspects of rope jumping can also develop the internal dialogue needed to establish basic reading skills. Beat awareness and beat competency simulate the basic rhythm patterns of our language that need to be established for better language acquisition. Jumping to a beat or rhythm makes rope jumping an ideal tool for cultivating coordination and agility.

TIP

Coordination

Coordination can be described as precisely integrated muscle group responses to a demand for agile movement. Coordination is also critical to efficient movement in ways that can increase endurance and stamina. In addition, it reduces one's risk of injury—especially the types caused by stumbles and other flukes.

As a result, athletes, coaches, and trainers are willing to explore several strategies and techniques for improving foot work, eye–hand coordination, the ability to change direction efficiently, and performing other movements that require high levels of coordination. Indeed, coordination is required in a wide variety of sport-specific movements—for example, in American football, the footwork required of offensive linemen who execute complex blocking schemes. Coordination is also crucial for swimmers, who must synchronize each stroke with their breathing and kicking, and it is an obvious need for boxers and martial artists, who must execute precise, well-timed movements in a fraction of a second in order to secure a competitive advantage. In addition, track-and-field athletes are often required to demonstrate remarkable coordination while generating power in order to execute precise running, jumping, or throwing movements.

> **TIP**
>
> *The vestibular system that creates spatial awareness and mental alertness is strengthened through activities such as rope jumping. Balance and jumping activities also provide student athletes with a framework for reading and other academic skills.*

Rope jumping is one of few activities that can increase eye–hand–foot coordination as well as synchrony of the upper-body (torso) and lower-body muscle groups. Coordination gives you the ability to integrate other fitness components (e.g., strength, power, agility, balance, flexibility, and endurance) in ways that improve your performance, reduce energy system demands, and reduce your risk of injury.

Kinesthetic Awareness

As you develop through my jump rope system and programs, you will notice that you are making subtle adjustments in your posture to maximize your proficiency, balance, and endurance. These adjustments may include maintaining an erect posture and keeping your head squarely above your shoulders while focusing straight ahead. Such adjustments may kick in automatically, especially during sessions that test your anaerobic thresholds. They will also cultivate in you a monitoring style of attention—a special mental state practiced by many of the world's top athletes.

As your training continues, you will become more aware of how often you are applying the monitoring style of attention. No matter how proficient you become, rope jumping requires that you constantly monitor your execution, even if you focus only on the rhythm of the exercise. By monitoring your rope-jumping execution, you further develop the kinesthetic and proprioceptive senses that are critical to agility. The act of monitoring each movement helps your body make numerous subtle corrective neuromuscular adjustments that lead to longer periods of continuation (durations of jumping between catches of the rope) at higher levels of intensity and proficiency.

These developments take place even during missteps and catches of the rope as part of a feedback process in which you learn from both successes and mistakes. You are succeeding when you can execute your rope-jumping sets with precision and proficiency. The positive feedback says that you should keep doing what you are doing. As the saying goes, if it ain't broke, don't fix it! Your mistakes and missteps also give you good information. They tell you that you need to change something—perhaps make a subtle adjustment in your technique—such as turning the rope with your wrists rather than your arms, jumping just high enough to clear the rope, or making sure your posture is erect.

You may find yourself making slight adjustments within each jump rope set—even in those sets without catches or missteps. In any case, these adjustments will build your muscle memory and your jump rope proficiency as you enhance your kinesthetic awareness and proprioception. Because of the ever-present possibility of missteps during rope-jumping sessions, your attention expands to encompass all aspects of the activity, which includes your whole body. And as you increase your ability to recover from missteps and continue jumping—especially during complex routines—you further enhance your balance, coordination, and agility.

This ongoing process requires *constant application of the monitoring attention style* that facilitates subtle neuromuscular adjustments to sustain progressively longer periods of continuation at high levels of proficiency. These capabilities enable you to deliver improved sports performance while also cultivating a sense of gracefulness and fluidity in everyday physical movements. Thus, as an agility training tool, rope jumping helps your "body become all eyes" by enhancing your proprioception and heightening your kinesthetic awareness. These developments then manifest as significant improvements in your balance and rhythm.

Interval Circuit Training Programs

These programs should be executed only after you have mastered the basic rope-jumping skills and established both a jump rope capacity and a training baseline as follows:

1. At least *100 jumps in 30 seconds* using the alternate-foot step (counting the right foot only and multiplying by 2 to get the number of total jumps in the set)
2. At least *30 power jumps in 30 seconds*

You should reestablish your training baseline each week. It can take several years to reach your maximum baseline, so keep jumping to improve your proficiency and to attain progressively higher levels of fitness. As your jump rope proficiency, endurance, and intensity improve, so will your baseline score.

Tables 9.1 and 9.2 show sample pretests for establishing a training baseline for the circuit training program using the alternate-foot step and the basic power jump.

Table 9.1   Pretest Example 1: 30 Seconds

Time	Repetitions for alternate-foot step	Baseline score
Do three 30-second sprints.	Record your reps for each set (count right foot only and multiply by 2).	Add reps from all 3 sets, then divide by 3.
30 sec	50 jumps × 2 = 100	306 jumps ÷ 3 = 102 (baseline)
30 sec	52 jumps × 2 = 104	
30 sec	51 jumps × 2 = 102	

Table 9.2   Pretest Example 2: 60 Seconds

Time	Repetitions for power jump	Baseline score
Do three 60-second sprints.	Record your reps for each set.	Add reps from all 3 sets, then divide by 3.
60 sec	100 jumps × 2 = 200	612 jumps ÷ 3 = 204 (baseline)
60 sec	104 jumps × 2 = 208	
60 sec	102 jumps × 2 = 204	

INTERVAL CIRCUIT TRAINING PROGRAM 1: SPEED, POWER, AND FINESSE

In-season

Use the underarm standard measurement. In order to correctly measure results, wait 1 week before you consider shortening the rope.

All 15 basic techniques

Training routine	Phase 1: Perform all sports cross-training jumps in chapter 5 for a total of 6 minutes at 75-80% of MHR or 160-180 RPM. Phase 2: Rotate between the circuit stations 4 times for a total of 4 minutes.

Circuit stations
 	
• Station 1: Speed jumping
  Alternate-foot step and high step
• Station 2: Power jumping
  Power jumps (basic bounce, bell jump, forward straddle, side straddle, skier's jump)
 	
• Station 3: Finesse jumping
  Arm crossover and side swing jump
	Speed jumping, power jumping, finesse jumping
	
	Jump for 30 seconds, then do active rest for 30 seconds (jog in place).
	Jump for 30 seconds, then do active rest for 30 seconds (jog in place).
	
	Jump for 30 seconds, then do active rest for 30 seconds (jog in place).

Duration	10 minutes: 8 minutes jump time, 2 minutes rest time
Intensity for stations	Jump at 85-95+% of MHR or 180-220+ RPM.
Goal	To decrease your active rest period between stations

program

INTERVAL CIRCUIT TRAINING PROGRAM 2: BALANCE, COORDINATION, AND AGILITY

In-season

Use the underarm measurement in the beginning. In order to correctly measure results, wait 1 week before you consider reducing the rope length.

Alternate-foot step, arm crossover, bounce step, forward straddle, high step, side straddle, X-foot cross

Training routine (creating squares clockwise)	Do 4 bounce steps (stationary).
	Do 4 alternate-foot steps (moving forward).
	Do 4 bounce steps (stationary).
	Do 4 alternate-foot steps (moving to the right).
	Do 4 bounce steps (stationary).
	Do 4 alternate-foot steps (moving backward).
	Do 4 bounce steps (stationary).
	Do 4 alternate-foot steps (moving to the left).
	Do 4 bounce steps (stationary).
	Do 4 high steps (moving forward).
	Do 4 bounce steps (stationary).
	Do 4 high steps (moving to the right).
	Do 4 bounce steps (stationary).
	Do 4 high steps (moving backward).
	Do 4 bounce steps (stationary).
	Do 4 high steps (moving to the left).
	Do 4 bounce steps (stationary).
	Do 4 arm crossovers with alternating feet (moving forward).
	Do 4 bounce steps (stationary).
	Do 4 arm crossovers with alternating feet (moving to the right).
	Do 4 bounce steps (stationary).
	Do 4 arm crossovers with alternating feet (moving backward).
	Do 4 bounce steps (stationary).
	Do 4 arm crossovers with alternating feet (moving to the left).
	Do 4 bounce steps (stationary).
	Do 4 side straddles (moving forward).
	Do 4 bounce steps (stationary).

program

Training routine (creating squares clockwise)	Do 4 forward straddles (moving to the right). Do 4 bounce steps (stationary). Do 4 side straddles (moving backward). Do 4 bounce steps (stationary). Do 4 forward straddles (moving to the left). Do 4 bounce steps (stationary). Do 4 X-foot crosses (moving forward). Do 4 bounce steps (stationary). Do 4 forward straddles (moving to the right). Do 4 bounce steps (stationary). Do 4 X-foot crosses (moving backward). Do 4 bounce steps (stationary). Do 4 forward straddles (moving to the left). Rest for 10-30 seconds. Repeat this sequence 6 or 7 times.
Duration	Approximately 10 minutes: 8-9 minutes jump time, 1-2 minutes rest time
Intensity	Jump at 80+% of MHR (180+ RPM).
Goals	Using the different planes, jump in the pattern of a square for each of the 5 routines (moving clockwise) to improve your balance, coordination, and agility. Maintain the same speed from one technique to the next. Decrease your rest period between sets.

program

INTERVAL CIRCUIT TRAINING PROGRAM 3: BALANCE, COORDINATION, AND AGILITY

In-season

Use the underarm measurement in the beginning. In order to correctly measure results, wait 1 week before you consider reducing the rope length.

Alternate-foot step, arm crossover, bounce step, forward straddle, high step, side straddle, X-foot cross

Training routine	As a warm-up for the single-leg jumps to follow:
	Do 50 alternate-foot steps.
	Do 50 high steps.
	Do 50 alternate-foot steps.
	Do 50 high steps.
	Rest for 10-30 seconds.
	Do 4 alternate-foot steps.
	Do 4 high steps.
	Repeat until you have completed 100 jumps total.
	Rest for 10-30 seconds.
	Single-leg jumps:
	Do 20 bounce steps on right leg only (with left leg bent and knee at 90-degree angle).
	Do 20 bounce steps on left leg only (with right leg bent and knee at 90-degree angle).
	Repeat 5 times.
	Rest for 10-30 seconds.
	Creating an L shape:
	Do 4 skier's jumps (moving forward).
	Do 4 skier's jumps (moving backward).
	Do 4 bell jumps (moving to the right).
	Do 4 bell jumps (moving to the left).
	Repeat this sequence 4 or 5 times.
	Rest for 10-30 seconds.
	Do 4 X-foot crosses (moving forward).
	Do 4 X-foot crosses (moving backward).
	Do 4 forward straddles (moving to the right).
	Do 4 forward straddles (moving to the left).

program

Training routine	Repeat this sequence 4 or 5 times.
	Rest for 10-30 seconds.
	To increase kinesthetic awareness, jump with your eyes shut (basic bounce, both feet):
	Do 100 bounce steps.
	Do 100 alternate-foot steps.
	Do 4 bounce steps.
	Do 4 alternate-foot steps.
	Repeat until you have completed 100 jumps total.
Duration	Approximately 10 minutes: 7.5-9 minutes jump time, 1-2.5 minutes rest time
Intensity	Jump at 80%+ of MHR (180+ RPM).
	Note: Focus on technique rather than speed during single-leg jumps.
Goals	Use the different planes while executing complex foot movements to improve your balance, coordination, and agility.
	Maintain the same speed from one technique to the next.
	Decrease your rest period between sets.

program

How Skaters and NBA Players Use Rope Jumping to Improve Agility, Balance, and Coordination

Audrey K. Weisiger, two-time U.S. Olympic coach and former coach of Olympian Michael Weiss, uses rope jumping as part of the training and conditioning program for all of her young athletes. She is particularly impressed with how rope jumping increases her athletes' efficiency of movement.

Efficient movements allow athletes to conserve energy and employ it strategically while executing complex maneuvers. Because efficiency of movement streamlines energy expenditure, it leads to increases in endurance and stamina. Weisiger reports that rope jumping not only teaches her athletes how to jump properly, which prevents injury, but also teaches them to jump while keeping their torsos upright—a critical requirement for jumping in ice skates.

Sheila Thelen, master coach (Professional Skaters Association), executive director of Grassroots to Champions, international seminar presenter says:

As the number one figure skating seminar company in North America, we train thousands of skaters and coaches every year. One of our main presentations is "Buddy Lee's Jump Rope Training for Helping to Develop the Total Athlete." Working with skaters at the beginner level up through national and international competitive skaters, we teach the importance of the Buddy Lee rope system in their daily training regimens as a way to improve their agility on the ice, their balance and coordination, and their timing and rhythm for explosive jumps. At the Grassroots to Champions (G2C) seminars, we have introduced the Buddy Lee system to a number of top athletes who now train with it on a daily basis. They include Kiri Baga (2009 U.S. Novice Ladies Champion), Kate Charbonneau (2009 Canadian Junior Ladies National Champion), and Tommy Steenberg (top 10 skater in the U.S. Senior Men's Division). I'm sure that *many* future figure skating stars will be helped by the G2C platform of education infused with Buddy Lee's jump rope training system. We thank Buddy for his great system and the ongoing results it has provided.

And Jason Otter, NBA trainer, world-renowned basketball performer, and owner of Otter's School of Basketball reports:

Combining Buddy Lee's jump rope training with applied exercise science principles has given us one of the most useful tools for developing foot speed and agility in our clients—from the NBA level all the way down to our elite prep players. I have been involved with jump rope technology and Buddy Lee products for over five years now and have integrated his jump rope training system into four videos that teach dribbling drills and techniques for superior dribbling skills. I would recommend the Buddy Lee system to anyone, from the elite athlete to the weekend warrior.

Condition for Specific Sports and Fitness Goals

Rope jumping is a total-body exercise that can improve your performance in sports. Recent research in fitness and sports performance has supported my belief that high-intensity interval training is the key to achieving the high levels of anaerobic conditioning that are often crucial to gaining a competitive edge in most sports. In addition, fitness experts are now touting high-intensity interval training as an effective strategy for increasing the post-workout level of fat burning. And other researchers have found that high-intensity interval training also boosts cognitive functioning (e.g., producing improvements in memory and learning). One way—indeed, an ideal way—to perform high-intensity interval training is through rope jumping.

Rope jumping also offers great flexibility. You can continuously adapt your jump rope training programs to challenge your anaerobic thresholds and increase your related training and performance effects. Rope jumping is a simple exercise that simulates a wide range of speeds, changes of direction (particularly foot movements), and energy system usages that are typical of both slow- and fast-paced sports. Simulation is the key to identifying programs that will help you quickly reach your fitness and training goals.

You should complete my 3-step program before you start your sport-specific training: (1) master basic rope-jumping skills, (2) establish sufficient jump rope endurance, and (3) add anaerobic intensity. Your efforts to achieve extended training benefits will be based on intensity level (revolutions per minute, or RPM) and continuation. You will be unable to sustain high levels of RPM for up to 2 minutes if you have not developed sufficient rope-jumping capacity and proficiency. This is especially important during the sports training phase; if you have not developed adequate capacity and proficiency, you may be unable to adequately use the techniques that simulate sport-specific movements.

I emphasize two principles of simulation. First, I have designed these programs to draw upon your anaerobic energy systems in timed intervals that match the energy demands of sports performance. Consider this an application of the principles of high-intensity interval training. For example, sports such as football rely almost exclusively upon anaerobic energy systems. This is the case because each play lasts for just a few seconds (few plays last as long as 10 seconds). Each play is generally followed by a resting interval of 40 seconds, after which the athlete must be prepared to exert maximum effort during the next play. Therefore, a football player should use these performance demands to modify the jump rope programs presented in this book. One way to do so would be to repeat the following sequence for up to 5 minutes: 10 to 30 seconds of power jumping, followed by 30 seconds of a relaxed bounce step, followed by 10 to 30 more seconds of sprint jumping. Other sports with performance intervals (e.g., basketball) can also be simulated by my jump rope training programs. Endurance sports and some others require long-term use of the aerobic and fat-burning energy systems, which can best be simulated at intensity levels of 120 to 140 RPM.

Boxers and other fighters can tailor rope-jumping programs to simulate 2- to 4-minute rounds of competition, as well as the rest intervals between rounds. Tennis players can simulate the duration of rallies and the rest periods between points, games, and sets. I recommend that you conduct training sets—that is, intervals—at high-intensity levels to simulate the energy system demands of most sports, including the influence of competitive stress upon the body during sports performance.

Endurance athletes can train with sets that include up to 10 minutes of continuation at lower levels of intensity—for example, 160 RPM—because their sports (e.g., triathlons, cross-country skiing) generally require a capacity for extended aerobic and fat-burning performance. Golfers, whose rounds can last several hours, should also train with long periods of continuation at aerobic or fat-burning intensity levels to improve their overall conditioning. In fact, rope jumping can be especially beneficial for golfers, given their extreme need for eye–hand coordination, timing, and balance.

Swimmers should train with power jumps and at intensity levels up to 220 RPM because of the high anaerobic demands of their sport; swimming also makes great upper-body demands, and swimmers can use rope jumping to increase the strength and endurance of their shoulders, back, and arms. To best simulate the extreme anaerobic energy demands of this sport, I recommend that swimmers include multiple sets of 60 to 120 seconds at maximum RPM with no more than 1 minute of rest between sets. Training sessions should include power jump techniques.

Increasing the number of turns of the rope per jump is a way to quickly tax the anaerobic energy system and therefore derive increased training benefits.

Baseball players and racquet sport athletes (including table tennis and badminton players) should include rope-jumping techniques that emphasize high intensity—that is, RPM levels approaching 220 turns per minute—for shorter durations of time (perhaps 30 seconds), followed by 30 to 45 seconds at 140 to 160 RPM, for 5 minutes of continuous jumping per set. Often, this kind of sport features long periods of recovery, which should be simulated by integrating extended periods of low-intensity rope jumping into your training sessions. For more information on specific programs for these and other sports, see the charts included at the end of this chapter.

My second principle of simulation is that I have tailored my programs particularly to mimic the important movements of sports play. A sprinter's program, for example, should emphasize foot speed, balance, and anaerobic exertion. A skater's program, in contrast, should focus on agility, balance, and grace. A boxer's program should stress lightning-fast reflexes and quickness of the hands and feet. Boxers should train at high levels of intensity for 2 or more minutes to simulate the energy system demands of boxing rounds; each set should be followed by a 1- or 2-minute rest period to simulate the timed breaks between boxing rounds.

Whatever your sport, its particular energy system demands and its sport-specific movements will determine which techniques or combinations of techniques you should use in your jump rope training program (see table 10.1). Your program should simulate ideal performances; in

Table 10.1 The Energy System Demands of Specific Sports

Energy system	Intensity	Time	Sports
ATP-PC	High	0-30 sec	Badminton, baseball, boxing, cheerleading, diving, extreme sports, field hockey, football, gymnastics, judo, lacrosse, martial arts, mixed martial arts, Olympic lifting, powerlifting, racquetball, rugby, soccer (sprints), softball, squash, swimming (sprint), table tennis, tennis, track sprints (100 and 200 meters), track-and-field events (high jump, javelin, long jump, pole vault, shot put), volleyball, wrestling
Lactic acid	Moderate	30 sec-3 min	Ballet, basketball, bodybuilding, dance, figure skating, handball, hockey, in-line skating, speedskating, strength training, swimming (middle distance), track sprints (400, 600, 800 meters, 1000 meters dash, 1 mile), water polo
Aerobic	Low	3+ min	Archery, bowling, field hockey, general fitness, golf, lacrosse, running (long distance), shooting, swimming (distance)

other words, modify your training routine to simulate the movement and energy demands of the perfect performance.

Athletes in sports that require explosive movements, sprints, or vertical acceleration should emphasize power jumping techniques. Those in sports that require omnidirectional movements during rapidly changing situations should incorporate agility programs. Sprinters and runners should emphasize the alternate-foot step and high-step jumping techniques, which simulate running and sprinting at durations and intensity levels that can match ideal performances in these sports.

In addition, most athletic movements are part of, or are preceded by, some form of jumping that can be simulated by numerous techniques presented in this book. These include the explosive side-to-side movements of a tennis player, the artful dodging of a football running back, the rapid pivots of a basketball player, and the explosive spring of a wrestler. Power jumps can also be used to simulate sequences of strokes for swimmers. The point is that if you carefully examine your athletic movements, you will see how these movements, or phases of movements, can be simulated through one or more techniques in my jump rope training programs.

Rope Jumping During Off-Season, Preseason, and In-Season Training

You should use my preparatory 3-step conditioning program (presented in chapters 3, 4, and 5) in the off-season in order to save valuable sports training time during the preseason and in-season periods. Learning the 3-step system during the off-season provides a safe and smooth transition to learning high-intensity jump rope training workouts. More important, the conditioning program enables you to attain basic jump rope fitness and the ability to perform specific techniques that make up the more advanced, higher-intensity jump rope workouts.

Once you have completed the 3-step preparatory program, you should use the more concerted jump rope conditioning programs presented in chapter 6 and later chapters only during the preseason and in-season training cycles. Integrating a jump rope training program into your seasonal training cycles improves your sports training performance and helps you meet your fitness goals. Depending on your fitness level, my progressive 3-step jump rope conditioning program may take a few months, but you will notice gradual improvements in your athletic performance and fitness. In particular, you can use rope jumping to enhance your cardiovascular fitness. Depending on the time of season, you can integrate rope jumping on a daily basis as a warm-up before doing stretching exercises; it can also be included as a conditioning tool before or after practice (see chapter 12 for information on how rope jumping can be used for rehab conditioning). Rope jumping can also be used to increase blood circulation to all major muscle groups and as an efficient warm-up for precompetition stretching exercises.

Off-Season

The off-season is the best time to learn how to jump rope, develop jump rope proficiency, and build a solid aerobic foundation. To achieve maximum benefit, I suggest that you use my jump rope training as a separate workout from your other exercises in order to focus on and master my 3-step system. Choose an environment that provides sufficient space, a good jumping surface, and the opportunity to jump to your favorite music. Jumping to your music or to a beat helps you develop timing and rhythm for successful jumping.

The off-season is also a good time to learn techniques that simulate key movements in your sport. It is best to incorporate these techniques into your jump rope regimen after you develop a basic jump rope capacity and establish a reliable baseline.

The off-season is considered the best time for athletes to recover from fatigue and injuries. It also provides an opportunity for you to acquire knowledge that you can use to improve your future sports performances. Therefore, you should take advantage of the off-season to do the following:

> **T**rain with the rope in the way you want to move and play when performing your sport. If you combine simulated sport-specific movements with cycles that simulate the energy demands of your sport, you will achieve a synergistic effect that dramatically increases your fitness and sports performance.
>
> TIP

1. Learn the basic jump rope skills presented in chapter 3.
2. Work through the remaining 2 phases in the 3-step conditioning program (see chapters 4 and 5).
3. Incorporate the 26 jump rope training techniques presented in chapter 4 into your efforts to increase your jump rope proficiency and improve your overall cardiovascular conditioning.

It is important that you consider the off-season as an opportunity to improve your conditioning and learn new training techniques. The preseason is the best time to apply these techniques in ways that improve your conditioning and performance. This is especially true for rope-jumping techniques designed to enhance sports performance. Do not wait until the preseason to learn new techniques; rather, use it to improve your conditioning and performance.

Although rope jumping is a simple exercise, it is not necessarily easy. First-time jumpers may feel awkward and embarrassed, especially if they feel clumsy in the presence of other athletes or onlookers. Some people take longer than others to learn or develop proficiency in jump rope techniques. This is another reason that the off-season is the best time for learning how to jump rope. It gives you enough time to learn these techniques and develop the necessary levels of proficiency to incorporate the techniques into your preseason and in-season training and conditioning programs.

For athletes who have already developed high levels of rope-jumping proficiency and conditioning, the off-season can be used to further enhance fitness and performance levels. For example, these athletes can use rope jumping during the off-season to establish more demanding simulations of their sports movements and develop optimum levels of conditioning.

Athletes should also use the off-season to work on the specific strengths and weaknesses of their sports performance. Jumping rope up to 4 or 5 times a week is enough to develop a 10-minute basic jump rope capacity (see the sports training phase presented in chapter 5), which will prepare you for the basic warm-up and preconditioning sprint and power programs. Some athletes may challenge themselves with 15- to 30-minute rope-jumping training programs, especially if they have high levels of conditioning or participate in sports that require high levels of anaerobic-based stamina or endurance.

In any case, you should execute the jump rope conditioning programs only after you have mastered the basic jump rope skills, attained a jump rope capacity, and established a training baseline (pretest charts are included in chapters 5, 7, 8, and 9). You should be able to equal or improve your baseline score in each successive jump rope session.

Finally, the off-season can also be an excellent time to use rope jumping to manage your weight. See chapter 13 for more information on this use of rope jumping.

Off-Season Rope Jumping

During this developmental stage, learn the skill of jumping and work on increasing your jump rope capacity.

- Master the skill of jumping (see chapter 3 discussion of the base phase of the 3-step conditioning program).
- Develop a jump rope capacity (see chapter 4 discussion of the conditioning phase).
- Increase your jump rope intensity (see chapter 5 discussion of the sports training phase).
- Establish a baseline for measuring your jump rope intensity (see chapter 5).
- Implement the preconditioning programs.
- Identify and practice the jump rope techniques that simulate the movement and energy system demands of your sport.
- Integrate these sport-specific techniques into your conditioning program.

Frequency: 4 or 5 times per week as a conditioner

Duration: 10 minutes total for novice jumpers; up to 30 minutes for highly conditioned athletes who have already established high levels of rope-jumping capacity or proficiency; 2 or more minutes of continuation at 180 to 220 RPM

Intensity: 70 to 85 percent of maximum heart rate (MHR); 85 to 95 percent of MHR for highly conditioned athletes who have already established high levels of rope-jumping proficiency

Preseason

The greatest benefits of my jump rope training programs will take place during the preseason at the beginning of your sport's practice. An athlete's training regimens should simulate his or her sport in form, content, and intensity levels so that he or she can be ideally prepared for sports competition. Preseason jump rope training enhances your fitness level, reflexes, motor skills, balance, and coordination to help prevent injuries and gives you a safe and smooth transition into in-season training. During the preseason, you should progress from the initial stages of developing rope-jumping proficiency into the basic, intermediate, and advanced jump rope programs. Doing so requires jumping in sessions of 10 minutes or more at least 4 times per week, which will produce the necessary improvements in cardiovascular fitness for you to deliver high levels of in-season sports performance. It is important to challenge yourself to meet the highest possible levels of proficiency during the preseason; this should be your focus for preseason jump rope training. Then, during in-season training, you will be challenged to maintain or sustain your highest level of proficiency. I also advise that you continue to use the warm-up routines before in-season sports training practices or competitions.

Preseason Rope Jumping

During the preseason, jump to simulate your sport in form, content, and intensity. Perform your jump rope programs at the beginning of sports training practice. This approach catches you at a fresh start where you can exert maximum effort with full concentration and implement correct technique; it also serves as an excellent warm-up and transition into sports play.

- Establish a new baseline for measuring your jump rope intensity.
- Implement the basic and intermediate programs.
- Continue to use the warm-up routines.

Frequency: 4 or 5 times per week as an aerobic and anaerobic conditioner

Duration: 5 to 10 minutes total for most athletes (endurance athletes can jump for longer periods)

Intensity: 85 to 95 percent of MHR with 10- to 30-second bursts at 95+ percent of MHR (highly conditioned athletes can attempt 95+ percent MHR exertion for up to 2 minutes)

My training programs generate anaerobic stress levels similar to those created by resistance and high-intensity interval training. For example, jump rope training features high levels of repetitive movements that can result in your experiencing buildup of lactic acid in your shoulders, forearms, calves, or quadriceps after a session of sprint, agility, or power training. It is also quite possible that some athletes may experience delayed muscle soreness after high-intensity jump rope training.

You should do plenty of stretching (10 to 20 minutes) over the course of each jump session to aid recovery. Allow 24 hours of rest between high-intensity and power jump sessions. Ideally, my sprint, power, and circuit training programs should be executed on off-days from resistance and endurance training programs.

If my programs are executed according to these guidelines, you will notice significant gains in speed, quickness, agility, explosiveness, and overall conditioning that will complement your other training programs. You will also develop an anaerobic fitness level that can be easily maintained throughout your sport's season.

In-Season

Athletes should strive to reach their fitness goals during the preseason and maintain that level of fitness during the in-season period. Athletes can sustain peak conditioning levels by using advanced jump rope training programs as a conditioner 2 or 3 times per week after practice. They can also use 5-minute jump rope routines as a warm-up before daily practice or sports competition.

Many athletes continue actively training to improve performance areas in their sport well into the in-season period, and they can continue using my training programs as well. However, given the typical wear and tear on the body during sports competitions, programs should be modified to accommodate the need for critical recovery time after competitive events.

Therefore, athletes should reduce their high-intensity jump rope training sessions to no more than 3 sessions per week during seasonal competition to allow for adequate recovery time. Reduced training frequency further accommodates the need for additional rest required of fatigued bodies as the season winds down. But during state, national, or world-qualifying tournament time, athletes can still jump rope daily as a warm-up before stretching and as a transition into sports play.

The goal of in-season training is to maintain the athletic proficiency and cardiovascular fitness levels that result in sustained sports performance. Jump rope conditioning sessions should be short, intense, and sport-specific. Integrate only one advanced conditioning program per session during in-season sports practices. Do not overtrain—excessive jump rope training can negatively affect sports performance and impinge upon critical recovery and in-season training routines. Anaerobic training can quickly deplete glycogen levels and increase catabolism (i.e., protein or muscle breakdown). These effects are important to building or increasing conditioning, but they can have negative effects during the in-season period—a time when recovery can be just as critical as training in order to maintain high levels of sports performance.

In-Season Rope Jumping

As the season progresses into sports competition, keep your jump rope training sessions short and intense to maintain training effects while minimizing the risk of overtraining. You can perform the warm-up jump rope programs at the beginning of sports training practice; incorporate advanced conditioning programs after your sports training practice. You should reach your peak aerobic and anaerobic fitness levels during the preseason, then strive to maintain these conditioning levels throughout the in-season period.

- Maintain established preseason baseline.
- Continue using the advanced-level programs to maintain preseason conditioning.
- Focus upon sport-specific rope-jumping techniques during in-season training as part of your warm-up routines.
- Continue to use the warm-up routines before training sessions and sports competitions.

Integrate advanced-level programs at the end of sports practices for the winning edge. Doing so pushes you to use perfect technique and efficient movements despite fatigue and prepares you both physically and mentally for overtime competitions. This is the championship edge that can make the difference between gold, silver, and bronze.

Frequency: 2 or 3 times per week as an anaerobic conditioner; daily warm-up routines before sport-specific training, jump rope training, or sports competition.

Duration: 5 minutes per session for most athletes (no more than 10 minutes per session for endurance athletes)

Intensity: 85 to 95 percent of MHR with 10- to 30-second bursts at 95+ percent of MHR (no more than two 2-minute bursts at 95+ MHR or up to 220 RPM in any single training session)

Sport-Specific Programs

You will find specific advice for tailoring a jump rope regimen to meet your sport or exercise goals on the following pages. Find your sport in the charts to see discussion of benefits, recommendations, and suggestions for seasonal training. Continue to use the warm-up programs throughout all seasons. Keep in mind that you can use the warm-up programs presented in chapter 11 whenever you are warming up. In addition, I often recommend using them during the in-season period, since at that point you are maintaining your conditioning level from the intense competition.

Program Index

This list includes jump rope programs referred to in the following chart of sport-specific regimens; it indicates the pages where they can be found.

Sport-Specific Programs

General fitness	
Primary energy system	Aerobic (3+ min)
Developmental focus of rope jumping	• Efficiently warms the muscles in the upper and lower body before stretching exercises and weight training. • Helps develop aerobic capacity in one-third of the time other exercises take. • Tones and trims arms, legs, gluteals, and waistline as well as upper body. • Aids in weight loss. • Serves as a cool-down after exercise to lower respiration. • Serves as an active-rest exercise between weightlifting sets.
Recommendations and suggested jump rope techniques	• Focus on mastering the basic bounce and alternate-foot step. • Incorporate the high step to work the stomach, firm the buttocks, and shape the legs. • Incorporate the X-foot cross to trim the inner and outer thigh muscles. • Perform warm-up programs at the low end of the aerobic zone (70%) for weight loss, for active rest, and to cool down. • Perform programs at the high end of the aerobic zone (80%) to improve cardiovascular fitness.
Suggested programs (no season required)	• 3-step conditioning program • Endurance program levels 1 and 2 • Endurance program level 3 for weight loss
Strength training, bodybuilding	
Primary energy system	Lactic acid (30 sec-3 min)
Developmental focus of rope jumping	• Efficiently warms the muscles in the upper and lower body before stretching exercises and weight training. • Aids in weight loss as well as for cutting weight prior to a competition. • Provides heart with rhythmic steady exercise during heavy strength training cycles. • Aims to improve anaerobic fitness levels to decrease rest time between sets. • Serves as an effective warm-up, cool-down, and active rest between weightlifting sets. • Conditions shoulder and leg muscles to aid recovery from lifting.
Recommendations and suggested jump rope techniques	• Focus on mastering the basic bounce and alternate-foot step. • Perform warm-up programs at the low end of the aerobic zone at 70% when losing weight, for active rest and cool down. • Perform programs at the high end of the aerobic zone at 80% when used to improve cardiovascular fitness. • Jump rope as active rest between sets for one minute or 100 jumps.
Suggested programs	• 3-step conditioning program • Endurance program levels 1 and 2 • Endurance program level 3 for weight loss

(continued)

Olympic lifting, powerlifting

Primary energy system	ATP-PC (0-30 sec)
Developmental focus of rope jumping	• By improving aerobic fitness, rope jumping helps offset the pressure imposed on the heart by the Valsalva maneuver, in which a person tries to exhale forcibly without allowing air to exit through the mouth or nose. This maneuver is used during heavy weightlifting such as squatting and bench pressing. Provides the heart with rhythmic, steady exercise during heavy strength training cycles. • Improves anaerobic fitness levels to decrease rest time between sets. • Serves as an effective warm-up, cool-down, and means of active rest between weightlifting sets. • Conditions shoulder and leg muscles to aid recovery from lifting. • Even though the primary energy system here is the creatine phosphate, rope jumping does not aim to improve the strength and power required in these sports but serves as active rest and improves cardiorespiratory fitness.
Recommendations and suggested jump rope techniques	• The most important techniques are the basic bounce and the alternate-foot step. • Perform warm-up programs at the low end of the aerobic zone (70%) for weight loss, for active rest, and to cool down. • Perform programs at the high end of the aerobic zone (80%) to improve cardiovascular fitness.
Suggested programs	**Off-season:** • 3-step conditioning program **Preseason:** • Basic and intermediate warm-up programs • Endurance program level 2 **In-season:** • Advanced warm-up program

Boxing, martial arts, mixed martial arts, wrestling, judo

Primary energy system	Lactic acid (30 sec-3 min)
Developmental focus of rope jumping	• Develops hand and foot speed for punching, blocking, throwing, feinting, and making leg-sweeping movements in offensive and defensive takedowns and ground attacks. • Improves strength development of hip flexors, legs, knees, ankles, and feet for kicking and balancing while throwing, hooking legs, and doing sweeping movements. • Develops anaerobic energy for matching the high intensity of 3-minute rounds of nonstop fighting and aerobic energy for 12 rounds. • Develops eye-hand-foot coordination for proper awareness during landing, punching, kicking, and forearm and knee strikes. • Develops good balance and agility in reacting to punches, kicks, takedowns, and throws. • Develops muscular endurance in the arms, chest, and back for grappling, pulling, punching, blocking, and throwing.

Boxing, martial arts, mixed martial arts, wrestling, judo → *continued*	
Recommendations and suggested jump rope techniques	• Integrate full twister, high step, and bounding movements in warm-up programs. • Replace alternate-foot technique in sprint programs with the high step and side swing jump.
Suggested programs	**Off-season:** • 3-step conditioning program • Basic and intermediate sprint preconditioning programs • Basic and intermediate power preconditioning programs **Preseason:** • Basic power program • Basic sprint program • Intermediate sprint program • Interval circuit training program 1 **In-season:** • Advanced sprint programs • Advanced power programs

Gymnastics, cheerleading, diving	
Primary energy system	ATP-PC (0-30 sec)
Developmental focus of rope jumping	• Develops the maximal and submaximal vertical leap capability needed for acrobatic movements. • Conditions muscles in the lower body to build leg power and perform a continuous series of quick, explosive, high-elevation jumps. • Develops proprioception, strength, and endurance in the feet, ankles, knees, and legs for repetitive jumping, flipping, spinning, and landing movements, as well as push-off and rotational movements. • Reduces impact by using the lower extremities (feet, ankles, knees, and legs) as a buffer to absorb forces from continuous jumping. • Improves endurance and strength of hand and wrist muscles for eagle grip and over- and undergrips. • Conditions the muscles of the upper body for rotational trunk movements during diving.
Recommendations and suggested jump rope techniques	• Incorporate triple jumps in the power programs with a trampoline surface for improving vertical acceleration. • Use the power and triple jumps to improve vertical acceleration. • Concentrate on proper form and safe landings. • During power jump programs, incorporate the power side straddle, power forward straddle, power skier's jump, power bell jump, and power full twister.
Suggested programs	**Off-season:** • 3-step conditioning program • Basic and intermediate power preconditioning programs **Preseason:** • Basic power program • Intermediate power program • Interval circuit training programs 1, 2, and 3 **In-season:** • Advanced warm-up program • Advanced power programs

(continued)

Dance, ballet, figure skating

Primary energy system	Lactic acid (30 sec–3 min)
Developmental focus of rope jumping	• Develops the maximal and submaximal vertical leap capability needed for dance movements. • Develops leg, knee, ankle, and foot strength for repetitive jumping, flipping, spinning, and landing movements to minimize injuries. • Improves endurance and strength of hand and wrist muscles for hand movements. • Develops pivotal and rotational movements for skating, jumping, and spinning.
Recommendations and suggested jump rope techniques	• Incorporate triple-unders in the power programs with bounding surface. • Use the power and triple jumps to improve vertical acceleration. • Concentrate on proper form and safe landings. • During power jump programs, incorporate the power side straddle, power forward straddle, power skier's jump, power bell jump, and power full twister.
Suggested programs	**Off-season:** • 3-step conditioning program • Basic and intermediate sprint preconditioning programs • Basic and intermediate power preconditioning programs **Preseason:** • Intermediate sprint program • Intermediate power program • Interval circuit training programs 2 and 3 **In-season:** • Advanced warm-up program • Advanced power programs

Football, rugby, soccer

Primary energy system	ATP-PC (0–30 sec)
Developmental focus of rope jumping	• Develops footwork necessary to cover short and long distances very fast while avoiding tackles and obstacles. • Develops explosive power movements off the line, in the backfield, on kick off and returns, and after quick stops during the course of the game. • Develops agility for rapid and accurate changes in direction during pass patterns to catch or receive the ball and during running to evade tackles or defenders. • Develops eye-hand-foot coordination and body awareness when kicking, catching, or passing the ball. • Develops the speed, quickness, and agility that enable you to assess the game situation and react quickly while moving at top speed. • Develops leg, knee, ankle, and foot strength for preventing injuries. • Develops balance and coordination to maintain body control and posture when moving with or without the ball.

Recommendations and suggested jump rope techniques	• Incorporate the high step in place of the alternate-foot step. • Focus on 10-second sprints during jumping. • Although the primary energy system is creatine phosphate, these sports are performed in short bursts. A well-trained aerobic base allows you to sustain high intensity throughout the game. • Jump for durations of 15-30 minutes to build aerobic capacity; integrate short bursts of high intensity for 10-15 seconds.
Suggested programs	**Off-season:** • 3-step conditioning program • Basic and intermediate sprint preconditioning programs • Basic and intermediate power preconditioning programs **Preseason:** • Basic and intermediate sprint programs • Intermediate power program • Interval circuit training program 1 • Endurance program levels 1 and 2 **In-season:** • Advanced warm-up program • Advanced power programs • Advanced sprint programs

Baseball, softball	
Primary energy system	ATP-PC (0-30 sec)
Developmental focus of rope jumping	• Develops eye-hand-foot coordination for hitting, pitching, catching, and throwing the ball. • Improves aerobic endurance to prevent fatigue in shoulder and arm muscles for hitting, throwing, pitching, and catching. • Develops high levels of anaerobic fitness for sprinting around bases, catching the ball, and making plays. • Develops rotational and pivotal hip movements for batting and pitching. • Improves footwork and agility for reacting instantly to playing situations. • Improves hand and wrist strength for grabbing, catching, and throwing.
Recommendations and suggested jump rope techniques	• Incorporate arm movements with the arm side swing and arm crossover for eye-hand coordination. • Focus on 10-second sprints during jumping.
Suggested programs	**Off-season:** • 3-step conditioning program • Basic and intermediate sprint preconditioning programs • Basic and intermediate power preconditioning programs **Preseason:** • Basic sprint program • Interval circuit training program 1 **In-season:** • Advanced warm-up program • Advanced sprint programs • Jumping before each practice

(continued)

(continued)

Tennis, badminton	
Primary energy system	ATP-PC (0-30 sec)
Developmental focus of rope jumping	• Helps develop high levels of aerobic and anaerobic endurance for conditioning muscles of the whole body to help maintain good technique, balance, and body control throughout the game. • Improves timing, rhythm, and hip and pelvic rotation for striking forces to perform horizontal and vertical swinging actions. • Improves endurance in hands, wrists, and arms for improved grip and racket control. • Conditions the legs to perform a series of low-elevation jumps combined with submaximal-elevation jumps for serving, striking, and returning the ball or shuttle. • Improves hand and foot speed and footwork necessary for recognizing situations and reacting instantaneously during high-intensity play. • Develops proprioception of ankles and feet to reduce risk of injuries.
Recommendations and suggested jump rope techniques	• Incorporate the power jump, skier's jump, side straddle, and bell jump for improving agility. • Incorporate arm side swing and arm crossover to mimic fast hand movements of serving, returning, and hitting the ball or shuttle. • Be sure to travel while jumping with different techniques.
Suggested programs	**Off-season:** • 3-step conditioning program • Basic and intermediate sprint preconditioning programs • Basic and intermediate power preconditioning programs **Preseason:** • Intermediate sprint program • Intermediate power program • Endurance program levels 1, 2, and 3 **In-season:** • Advanced warm-up program • Advanced sprint programs • Advanced power programs • Interval circuit training programs 2 and 3

Table tennis, racquetball, squash	
Primary energy system	Lactic acid (30 sec-3 min)
Developmental focus of rope jumping	• Helps develop high levels of aerobic and anaerobic endurance for conditioning muscles of the whole body to help maintain good technique, balance, and body control throughout the game. • Improves timing, rhythm, and hip and pelvic rotation for striking forces to perform horizontal and vertical swinging actions. • Improves endurance in hands, wrists, and arms for improved grip and racket control. • Conditions the legs to perform a series of low-elevation jumps combined with submaximal-elevation jumps for serving, striking, and returning the ball. • Improves hand and foot speed and footwork necessary for recognizing situations and reacting instantaneously during high-intensity play. • Develops proprioception of ankles and feet to reduce risk of injuries.
Recommendations and suggested jump rope techniques	• Incorporate the power jump, skier's jump, side straddle, and bell jump for improving agility. • Use all planes—forward, backward, and lateral—to simulate sport movements.
Suggested programs	**Off-season:** • 3-step conditioning program • Basic and intermediate sprint preconditioning programs • Basic and intermediate power preconditioning programs • Endurance program level 1 **Preseason:** • Intermediate sprint program • Intermediate power program • Interval circuit training programs 2 and 3 • Endurance program level 2 **In-season:** • Advanced warm-up program • Advanced sprint programs • Advanced power programs • Interval circuit training program 1

(continued)

Field hockey, lacrosse	
Primary energy system	ATP-PC (0-30 sec) and aerobic (3+ min)
Developmental focus of rope jumping	• Improves aerobic fitness levels to improve recovery time between plays. • Improves agility for rapid and accurate directional change in offensive play while avoiding defensive movements. • Improves body awareness and eye-hand-foot coordination for striking and throwing objects while moving. • Develops hand grip, forearm strength, and endurance for improved stick control. • Improves endurance in shoulders and arms for striking and throwing muscles.
Recommendations and suggested jump rope techniques	• Incorporate some side straddles, skier's jumps, and X-foot crosses for lateral shifting in the sprint programs. • Incorporate arm side swings and arm crossovers for enhanced hand and stick speed. Use all planes when jumping. • Integrate bouts of high-intensity jumping with running, bounce step, and side and forward straddles.
Suggested programs	**Off-season:** • 3-step conditioning program • Basic and intermediate sprint preconditioning programs • Basic and intermediate power preconditioning programs **Preseason:** • Intermediate sprint program • Basic power program • Interval circuit training programs 2 and 3 • Endurance program levels 2 and 3 **In-season:** • Advanced sprint programs • Interval circuit training program 1
Basketball, handball	
Primary energy system	Lactic acid (30 sec-3 min)
Developmental focus of rope jumping	• Develops eye, hand, and foot coordination, balance, and body awareness for striking, blocking, dunking, dribbling, and shooting skills. • Improves agility for quickness on and off the ball while maintaining good form and control. • Develops proprioception, strength, and endurance in the feet, ankles, knees, and legs for jumping, stopping, starting, pivoting, rotating, and making movements (lateral, forward, and backward). • Reduces impact by using the lower extremities (feet, ankles, knees, legs, hips, and lower back) as a buffer to absorb forces from continuous jumping movements over the course of the game. • Conditions the muscles of the upper body for rotational trunk movements when passing, shooting, and striking. • Develops wrist and hand strength and endurance for catching, grabbing, dribbling, passing, and striking the ball for long periods of time. • Improves vertical acceleration and agility on the court.

Basketball, handball ➜ *continued*	
Recommendations and suggested jump rope techniques	• Perform all of the basic techniques. • Use power jumps to improve vertical acceleration. • During power jump programs, incorporate the power side straddle, power forward straddle, power skier's jump, power bell jump, and power full twister.
Suggested programs	**Off-season:** • 3-step conditioning program • Basic sprint program • Basic power program • Endurance program level 1 **Preseason:** • Intermediate sprint program • Intermediate power program • Endurance program level 2 **In-season:** • Interval circuit training program 1 • Advanced sprint programs • Advanced power programs

Volleyball	
Primary energy system	ATP-PC (0-30 sec)
Developmental focus of rope jumping	• Develops eye, hand, and foot coordination, balance, and body awareness for striking, setting, serving, blocking, and spiking skills. • Develops proprioception, strength, and endurance in the feet, ankles, knees, and legs for jumping, stopping, starting, pivoting, rotating, and making movements (lateral, forward, and backward). • Reduces impact by using the lower extremities (feet, ankles, knees, legs, hips, and lower back) as a buffer to absorb forces from continuous jumping movements over the course of the game. • Conditions muscles in the lower body to build leg power and perform a continuous series of quick, explosive, high-elevation jumps. • Conditions the muscles of the upper body for rotational trunk movements when passing and striking. • Develops wrist and hand strength and endurance for digging, passing, and striking the ball for long periods of time. • Improves vertical acceleration.
Recommendations and suggested jump rope techniques	• Perform all basic techniques. • Use power jumps to improve vertical acceleration. • During power jump programs, incorporate the power side straddle, power forward straddle, power skier's jump, power bell jump, and power full twister.

(continued)

(continued)

Volleyball ➜ *continued*	
Suggested programs	**Off-season:** • 3-step conditioning program • Basic and intermediate power preconditioning programs • Basic power program **Preseason:** • Interval circuit training programs 2 and 3 • Intermediate power program **In-season:** • Advanced warm-up program • Interval circuit training program 1 • Advanced power programs

Track (100 m sprint and hurdles)

Primary energy system	ATP-PC (0-30 sec)
Developmental focus of rope jumping	• Improves balance and body awareness during sprinting. • Develops explosive first steps for start speed and power off the blocks in sprinting events. • Improves speed by simulating the sprint running step and increases stride length and leg, hip, ankle, and foot strength. • Develops anaerobic fitness to improve sprint speed. • Develops hand and foot coordination.
Recommendations and suggested jump rope techniques	• Use the high step to improve sprinting stride and simulate the leg movements of sprinting and hurdling. • Focus on 10-second sprints during jumping.
Suggested programs	**Off-season:** • 3-step conditioning program • Basic and intermediate sprint preconditioning programs • Basic and intermediate power preconditioning programs **Preseason:** • Interval circuit training programs 2 and 3 • Intermediate sprint program • Intermediate power program **In-season:** • Advanced warm-up program • Advanced sprint programs • Advanced power programs

Track (400 and 800 m sprint and hurdles)

Primary energy system	Lactic acid (30 sec-3 min)
Developmental focus of rope jumping	• Improves balance and body awareness during sprinting. • Develops explosive first steps for start speed and power off the blocks in sprinting events. • Improves speed by simulating the sprint running step and increases stride length and leg, hip, ankle, and foot strength. • Develops anaerobic fitness to improve sprint speed. • Develops hand and foot coordination.
Recommendations and suggested jump rope techniques	• Use the high step to improve sprinting stride and simulate the leg movements of hurdling. • Focus on 20- and 30-second sprints during jumping.

Track (400 and 800 m sprint and hurdles) → *continued*

Suggested programs	**Off-season:**
	• 3-step conditioning program
	• Basic and intermediate sprint preconditioning programs
	• Basic and intermediate power preconditioning programs
	Preseason:
	• Interval circuit training program 1
	• Intermediate sprint program
	In-season:
	• Advanced warm-up program
	• Advanced sprint programs

Track-and-field events (high jump, javelin, long jump, pole vault, shot put)

Primary energy system	ATP-PC (0-30 sec)
Developmental focus of rope jumping	• Improves balance and body awareness during jumping events.
	• Develops explosiveness for jumps.
	• Develops upper-body momentum for events that involve throwing objects.
	• Improves speed by simulating the sprint running step and increases stride length and leg, hip, ankle, and foot strength.
	• Develops anaerobic fitness to improve sprint speed.
	• Develops gripping strength and endurance in the wrists and hands.
	• Develops hand and foot coordination.
Recommendations and suggested jump rope techniques	• Use the high step to improve sprinting stride.
	• Use power jumps to improve vertical acceleration.
Suggested programs	**Off-season:**
	• 3-step conditioning program
	• Basic and intermediate sprint preconditioning programs
	• Basic and intermediate power preconditioning programs
	Preseason:
	• Interval circuit training program 1
	In-season:
	• Advanced warm-up program
	• Advanced sprint programs
	• Advanced power programs

Long-distance running

Primary energy system	Aerobic (3+ min)
Developmental focus of rope jumping	• Develops endurance and acts as a low-impact substitute for running during inclement weather.
	• Improves speed by simulating the sprint running step and increases stride length and leg, hip, ankle, and foot strength.
	• Develops anaerobic fitness to improve sprint speed and decrease overall running time.
	• Develops hand and foot coordination.

(continued)

(continued)

Long-distance running → *continued*

Recommendations and suggested jump rope techniques	• Use the high step to improve sprinting stride; integrate bursts of high steps during endurance program work. • Use the alternate-foot step to train by traveling forward when jumping over the rope.
Suggested programs	**Off-season:** • 3-step conditioning program • Basic and intermediate sprint preconditioning programs • Endurance program levels 1, 2, and 3 **Preseason:** • Endurance program levels 4, 5, and 6 **In-season:** • Advanced warm-up program • Advanced sprint programs • Endurance program levels 3 and 4

Water polo

Primary energy system	Lactic acid (30 sec-3 min)
Developmental focus of rope jumping	• Develops anaerobic fitness for sprinting and endurance in the arms for stroking motions. • Develops rhythm and timing for better arm strokes. • Develops endurance in the wrists and hands for grasping the ball for long periods of time. • Develops upper- and lower-body endurance for stroking motions and treading water for long periods of time.
Recommendations and suggested jump rope techniques	• Focus on developing an anaerobic capacity for explosive movements while at the same time building an aerobic base to keep up your endurance throughout the game. • Integrate arm movements such as the arm crossover and arm side swing to improve gripping strength, muscular endurance in shoulders and arms for grabbing, catching, throwing, and blocking the ball.
Suggested programs	**Off-season:** • 3-step conditioning program • Basic and intermediate sprint preconditioning programs • Basic and intermediate power preconditioning programs **Preseason:** • Basic and intermediate sprint programs • Basic and intermediate power programs • Interval circuit training programs 2 and 3 • Endurance program level 1 **In-season:** • Interval circuit training program 1

Swimming (sprint)

Primary energy system	ATP-PC (0-30 sec)
Developmental focus of rope jumping	• Develops explosive start speed for pushing off the wall, board, or platform. • Develops anaerobic fitness for sprinting. • Develops rhythm and timing for better arm strokes. • Develops upper- and lower-body endurance for stroking motions.
Recommendations and suggested jump rope techniques	• Focus on developing an anaerobic capacity. • Use the high step technique during sprint programs.

Swimming (sprint) → *continued*	
Suggested programs	**Off-season:** • 3-step conditioning program • Basic and intermediate sprint preconditioning programs • Basic and intermediate power preconditioning programs **Preseason:** • Basic and intermediate sprint programs • Basic and intermediate power programs **In-season:** • Advanced sprint programs • Advanced power programs • Interval circuit training program 1

Swimming (distance)

Primary energy system	Aerobic (3+ min)
Developmental focus of rope jumping	• Develops aerobic fitness for endurance in the legs and arms for stroking and kicking motions. • Develops anaerobic fitness for sprinting to the finish line. • Develops rhythm and timing for better arm strokes. • Develops upper- and lower-body endurance for stroking motions.
Recommendations and suggested jump rope techniques	• Focus on developing an aerobic capacity. • Use high step technique during sprint programs.
Suggested programs	**Off-season:** • 3-step conditioning program • Basic and intermediate sprint preconditioning programs • Basic and intermediate power preconditioning programs • Endurance program levels 1, 2, and 3 **Preseason:** • Basic and intermediate sprint programs • Basic and intermediate power programs • Endurance program levels 4, 5, and 6 **In-season:** • Interval circuit training programs 2 and 3 • Endurance program level 1

Ice hockey

Primary energy system	Lactic acid (30 sec-3 min)
Developmental focus of rope jumping	• Develops agility for sudden changes of movement in all directions while assessing the game situation and avoiding opponents. • Develops explosive start movements. • Improves hand and foot coordination for striking the puck. • Improves gripping strength for better stick control. • Improves hand and foot quickness for offensive and defensive maneuvers while developing foot, ankle, and knee strength. • Helps you maintain balance during the constant shifting of body weight. • Improves rotational movements for skating and striking the puck.

(continued)

(continued)

Ice hockey → *continued*	
Recommendations and suggested jump rope techniques	• Incorporate power jumps into training for improving explosive movements, gripping strength, and stick control while skating. • Perform forward straddle, side straddle, skier's jump, bell jump, high step, and backward jumping for more efficient movements during skating.
Suggested programs	**Off-season:** • 3-step conditioning program • Basic and intermediate sprint preconditioning programs • Basic and intermediate power preconditioning programs **Preseason:** • Intermediate sprint program • Intermediate power program • Interval circuit training programs 2 and 3 **In-season:** • Advanced warm-up program • Interval circuit training program 1 • Advanced sprint programs • Advanced power programs

In-line skating, speedskating	
Primary energy system	Lactic acid (30 sec–3 min)
Developmental focus of rope jumping	• Develops speed. • Improves posture and stabilization of upper and lower body to defer fatigue. • Reduces body fat and increases lean muscle mass.
Recommendations and suggested jump rope techniques	• Use the alternate-foot step and high step to simulate sprinting motion and improve start speed while maintaining good balance during skating. • Use power jumps to improve muscular endurance and explosive takeoffs.
Suggested programs	**Off-season:** • 3-step conditioning program • Basic sprint preconditioning programs • Basic power preconditioning programs **Preseason:** • Basic and intermediate sprint programs • Basic and intermediate power programs **In-season:** • Advanced warm-up program • Advanced sprint programs • Advanced power programs

Golf, bowling, archery, shooting

Primary energy system	Aerobic (3+ min)
Developmental focus of rope jumping	• Conditions muscles of the shoulders, fingers, wrists, and hands for repetitive pulling and swinging movements. • Improves aerobic fitness for muscle relaxation, rhythm, timing, and controlled breathing during shooting, pulling, and swinging arm movements. • Develops endurance for maintaining relaxed breathing and concentration through long competition periods. • Develops eye, hand, and foot coordination, balance, and stability while maintaining good body position and timing for arm and hand releases. • Develops upper-body stability and balance during movements with an object in the hands.
Recommendations and suggested jump rope techniques	• Even though the primary energy system for these sports is aerobic, golfers can benefit from integrating arm side swings and arm crossovers in order to develop quick wrists and a more explosive golf swing. • The goal is to increase endurance for better muscle control, relaxation, and breathing, as well as sustaining the edge from beginning to finish.
Suggested programs	**Off-season:** • 3-step conditioning program **Preseason:** • Basic sprint program • Circuit training program 1 • Endurance program levels 1, 2, and 3 **In-season:** • Basic through advanced warm-up programs • Endurance program level 3

Extreme sports

Primary energy system	ATP-PC (30 sec-3 min)
Developmental focus of rope jumping	• Helps develop hand reaction time and footwork for reacting to sudden changes in direction while maintaining good balance. • Develops eye, hand, and foot coordination, as well as concentration and body control for proper awareness during jumping, leaping, falling, and spinning. • Develops hand and wrist strength and endurance for grasping for long periods of time. • Develops endurance for sustaining body control and concentration and maintaining high-performance play. • Conditions you to perform a series of low- to high-elevation jumps while maintaining body awareness and good balance.
Recommendations and suggested jump rope techniques	• Incorporate all techniques and use all planes (horizontal, lateral). • Use the high step in the sprint programs and use all jumps for better balance and agility.

(continued)

(continued)

Extreme sports ➜ *continued*	
Suggested programs	**Off-season:** • 3-step conditioning program • Basic and intermediate pre-sprint conditioning programs • Basic and intermediate power preconditioning programs **Preseason:** • Intermediate sprint program • Intermediate power program • Interval circuit training programs 2 and 3 **In-season:** • Advanced warm-up program • Advanced sprint programs • Advanced power programs • Interval circuit training program 1

A Physical Therapist's Opinion of Buddy Lee's System

I feel that Buddy Lee's approach to cross-conditioning for sports represents all the best of science, innovation, and practicality. He does not focus on rigid programming, equipment, or fitness trends. His focus is on the body (where the focus of all conditioning should start). He emphasizes timing, coordination, agility, body awareness, and body control. These elements provide both improved performance and injury prevention. These are also the words we use to describe the great ones. All great sports coaches have continuously maintained a focus on fundamentals (no matter how great or popular they may have become). I feel that Buddy represents the same fundamentals philosophy for conditioning. I consider him the expert in his field.

Gray Cook, MSPT, OCS, CSCS, Director of Orthopedic and Sports Physical Therapy at Dunn, Cook and Associates; Level One Olympic-style Weightlifting Coach; Instructor for the North American Sports Medicine Institute; Consultant to NFL, NBA, NHL and WNBA.

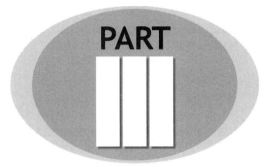

PART

III

SUPPLEMENTAL USES FOR JUMP ROPE TRAINING

Warm-Up, Cool-Down, and Active Rest

You can incorporate rope jumping into your regular training program as a warm-up, an active rest, or a cool-down. The portability of rope jumping makes this possible even during sports competitions; whereas other equipment, such as an exercise bike, generally requires access to a gym or fitness center, a jump rope takes just a few square feet of space and an adequate jumping surface. You can also use rope jumping as an effective part of your active rest phase during resistance training. It can keep your muscles warm while also activating your fat-burning and aerobic energy systems during intervals between anaerobic training sets.

Warming Up With the Jump Rope

You should warm up at almost the same intensity level of your sports performance in order to be properly prepared to engage in full-speed competition from the start. Most championship performances occur when you have an edge in time and space, and in some sports (e.g., wrestling) the start of the match can play a big role in the outcome. In my own case, warming up at a very high intensity level before each of my competitions played a crucial role in my competitive advantage on the mat and thus in my victories.

An effective warm-up program is the best way to increase your workout effectiveness and reduce your risk of injury. The best warm-up programs can also help you maximize your sports performance. Rope jumping offers an ideal warm-up before competition because it quickly engages all of your muscle groups, raises your core body temperature and heart rate, and fully activates your motor cortex—your brain's high-powered movement center.

Here are three programs (basic, intermediate, and advanced) by which you can use rope jumping as an effective warm-up before your sports competition or training session (each program is described in more detail near the end of this chapter):

1. In the basic warm-up program, you should jump at 60 to 65 percent of your maximum heart rate (MHR). You can use this program as a total-body warm-up before performing stretching exercises to prepare your muscles and help prevent injuries. It is best to stretch your muscles after you have warmed them up through several minutes of movement. Stretching cold muscles increases your risk of injury—particularly, pulled or strained muscles.

2. In the intermediate warm-up program, jump at 65 to 70 percent of your MHR. You can use this program as a warm-up for the high-intensity jump rope training programs presented in chapters 7, 8, and 9.

3. In the advanced warm-up program, jump at 70 to 80 percent of your MHR. You can use this program as a transition into full-speed sports play or competition. Rope jumping provides an effective warm-up for competitive advantages when performed at a heart rate close to that of full-speed sports play. Warming up at a higher intensity level before sports play also reduces the risk of injury in going from a resting state to all-out sports play. Your heart rate should be allowed to lower only to 70 percent of MHR from the time you ceased jumping to the moment you step into a full-speed sports practice or competition. This advanced warm-up program is sufficient to raise your heart rate to the level of full-speed sports play and competition.

Rope jumping is an especially useful exercise if your sport features short warm-up intervals. It quickly engages all your muscle groups in multijoint movements that provide an effective full-body warm-up in one-third of the time required by other aerobic-based routines. This rapid warm-up program frees you to engage in stretching or other preparations before your competition.

Although many coaches have recognized rope jumping as an effective warm-up program, they rarely use it as a safe and smooth transition into high-intensity sports performance. But once you have learned how to execute the warm-up programs presented in this chapter, you will be able to use them as a transition into a full-speed sports workout from the moment you arrive at your training site.

Upon reaching your training site, but before jumping rope, you can choose to begin warming up with a light form of stretching called pre-stretching. It consists of slow stretches, resembling a stretch that often accompanies a yawn, and provides a mental and physical boost for sports play and competition. Do each stretch (see pages 190-193) once and hold it for only a few seconds. This is your body's natural way of getting more oxygen to your brain, lungs, and muscles while also relieving stiffness and tension. Other pre-stretch benefits include increasing the blood flow to your shoulders, ankles, calves, knees, and quadriceps—the primary muscles and joints used in rope jumping. Pre-stretch movements are optional—not a requirement—but doing a pre-stretch followed by my jump rope warm-up program will ensure that your muscles are warmed up before you perform full stretching routines. Pre-stretching can also improve your joint mobility and increase the flexibility of your ligaments and tendons, and it allows you to immediately progress into rope jumping as a warm-up, cool-down, active-rest, or transitional exercise.

After pre-stretching, jump for 5 minutes to raise your core body temperature before you move on to a more complete stretching session that will reduce your risk of injury and prepare you for intense exercise, training, or competition. You can find the complete stretching session on pages 190-193.

Here are procedures for the three ways in which you can use rope jumping as a warm-up program:

Warm-Up for Stretching Exercises

1. Perform my basic warm-up program for 5 minutes at low intensity (140 revolutions per minute, or RPM).
2. Stretch all major muscle groups, especially your calves, for 10 to 20 minutes (see stretches on pages 191-193).
3. Hold each stretch for 20 seconds or longer.

Warm-Up for My High-Intensity Jump Rope Training Programs

1. Warm up with the intermediate warm-up program.
2. Execute the sprint, power, or circuit training program.

Transition Into Full-Speed Sports Play or Competition

1. Use my advanced warm-up program for 5 minutes to elevate your heart rate to 80 percent of your MHR
2. Go into a 30 second sprint to further raise your heart rate to match the intensity during sports play (85-95% of MHR).
3. For smooth transition into sports play, take 30-60 seconds to allow your heart rate to gradually go down until it approaches 70 percent of your MHR.

Active Rest With the Jump Rope

Active rest is a time period in which an athlete slows down, recovers, and rebuilds from intense workout or competition activity. It involves engaging in low-intensity exercise after a workout in order to improve blood circulation and hasten removal of lactic acid from the muscles while improving muscle recovery. Active rest also helps athletes prevent muscular injury and allows them to recover physically and psychologically from the stresses of training and competing while still maintaining a high fitness level. Rope jumping's portability and efficiency makes it an effective active-rest activity for many high-intensity sports. It can be used, for example, between sets of weightlifting, during breaks in sports training, and during breaks in competition.

Active rest comes in the following two forms:

1. During workout activity or breaks in sports competition
2. On days following competition or intense workouts

Here are some practical ways to use rope jumping for active rest between workouts and on recovery days:

Rope Jumping During Recovery Workouts

1. Between sets or during breaks in a workout or competition, jump for 1 minute at 100 to 180 RPM to maintain raised core body temperature. This minute of rope jumping may raise your heart rate to 70 percent of your MHR.
2. Rest for 30 to 60 seconds to allow your heart rate to slow down while your body remains prepared for the next burst of activity.

Rope Jumping on Recovery Days

1. On recovery days from sports training or competition, do a 10-minute session at 80 percent of your MHR.
2. Combine rope jumping and calisthenics as an effective method to maintain a high level of cardiovascular fitness and help remove lactic acid from your muscles for faster recovery.

Here is an example of a 10-minute recovery workout that combines various jump rope techniques with variations of push-ups and sit-ups.

1. Jump rope for 1 minute (combining the basic bounce and the alternate-foot step).
2. Do calisthenics for 1 minute (combining standard push-ups and standard sit-ups).
3. Jump rope for 1 minute (combining the side straddle and the forward straddle).
4. Do calisthenics for 1 minute (combining clapping push-ups and bicycle crunch). In the bicycle crunch, lie flat on the floor, with hands behind your head, while slowly going through a bicycle pedal motion, touching left knee to right elbow, then right knee to left elbow

5. Jump rope for 1 minute (combining the skier's jump and the bell jump).

6. Do calisthenics for 1 minute (combining decline push-ups and crunches).

7. Jump rope for 1 minute (combining the alternate-foot step and the high step).

8. Do calisthenics for 1 minute (combining diamond push-ups and twisting sit-ups). In the diamond push up, put your hands close together so the two index fingers and two thumbs are touching and form a diamond shape.

9. Jump rope for 1 minute (combining the arm crossover and the side swing jump).

10. Do calisthenics for 1 minute (combining incline push-ups and leg raises).

Reflecting on my wrestling career, I remember well how I would regularly warm up by jumping rope before each match, especially at national and world competitions. After jumping for a few minutes prior to a match, I would end with a 10-second sprint to match the target heart rate at which I expected to wrestle during the match. Then I would wait approximately 20 seconds to let my heart rate settle before stepping onto the mat.

Once on the mat to compete, I was a ball of energy, ready to explode, because my heart rate had already been in the target zone. It gave me an advantage over the competition and made it easier for me to score the first takedown without being overly winded. It also gave me the momentum to pin or superior-decision many of my opponents in the first 2 minutes.

At the 1993 National Greco-Roman Championships, I did just that, defeating my first three opponents by a pin or superior decision within the first 2 minutes. I had trained to win within the first 2 minutes because scoring first in world-class competition often makes the difference in gaining momentum, and it ultimately determined the outcome of these matches. I credit my explosive energy and momentum to my unique and sport-specific jump rope warm-up.

Cooling Down With the Jump Rope

A cool-down program performed after training or competition is just as important as your pretraining or precompetition warm-up. A cool-down program allows your body to readjust to the demands of normal physical activity. Your heart rate slows down so that your body can resume use of fat-burning rather than aerobic or anaerobic energy systems. This is important because while your body is in an aerobic or anaerobic state, your appetite becomes suppressed and you are less likely to feel the need to consume food, even though your body needs nutrition after intense training or competition. An effective cool-down program allows your body to make the physiological adjustments necessary for you to comfortably ingest food or a nutritional supplement that can immediately replace glucose and other nutrients used during training or competition.

You can use my basic warm-up program as an effective cool-down after training or competition. Afterward, remember to stretch all major muscle groups, especially your calves, to complete your cool-down.

Stretching for Flexibility

Gray Cook, a personal friend and the author of *Athletic Body in Balance*, talks about the importance of jump rope training and stretching exercises for developing symmetry and reducing the risk of injury in sports play. Gray explains that stretching is important to your training for many reasons—some less obvious than others. Stretching creates tension and elongation of muscle tissues, thus preparing them for action and stimulating neurological activity and blood flow. Stretching also provides critical feedback, informing you of whether or not a muscle or muscle group is strained or fatigued. If stretching produces muscle pain, you may have a serious injury and should seek medical attention. You should also seek medical care if stretching causes joint discomfort and not simply tension in a muscle group.

If your discomfort is due to general inflexibility, it is best to stretch your muscles slowly. Exhale while you extend your muscles and inhale while you contract them. Many people who are new to stretching actually contract the muscle they are trying to stretch without realizing what they are doing. Therefore, move slowly and allow a moderate degree of effort to stretch the muscle. Do not force your muscles to stretch beyond the level of moderate discomfort—a forced stretch can result in serious physical injury!

You can also use your stretching routine to check for overall body symmetry. Most stretches are performed on the left or right side of the body (for the extremities) or executed by movement toward or away from the spine. Either type of stretch allows you to determine symmetry—that is, to discern whether one part or side of your body is more flexible than its complement. If you observe differences in symmetry, target the area or part of your body that is less flexible and allow more time to stretch these muscles. Asymmetry can lead your body to compensate for inflexibility in ways that cause inefficient movements, waste energy, and increase your risk of injury. If you train asymmetrically (i.e., with left–right imbalance), you will move and compete asymmetrically. Improved symmetry, on the other hand, will allow you to jump rope with greater speed and proficiency. The stretches on the following pages will help you identify limitations and asymmetries in your overall body movements.

Follow these instructions for each stretch below:

1. Relax with each stretch, breathe deeply, and move slowly.
2. Exhale with each stretch and hold it for at least 20 seconds.
3. Repeat each stretch 3 to 4 times.
4. Stretch for a total of 10 to 20 minutes.

For more detailed information on stretching, see Gray Cook's *Athletic Body in Balance*. Here are a few stretches to help you get off to a safe and jumping start.

Hip Flexor Stretch

1. Kneel with your right foot forward, your left knee on the floor, and your left leg back.
2. Lean forward with your hips facing forward and your body upright (see figure 11.1).
3. Bend your right knee, but don't allow it to go over your toe, and contract your buttocks.
4. Repeat with your left leg.

Figure 11.1   Hip flexor stretch.

Seated Hamstrings and Calf Stretch

1. Inhale, exhale, and reach forward 6 inches (15 cm) above your left foot (so that your body forms a shape resembling the letter E). Lead with your chest and keep your kneecap and toe pointed upward (see figure 11.2).
2. Repeat with your right leg.

Figure 11.2   Seated hamstrings and calf stretch.

Standing Calf Stretch

1. Stand with your hands about shoulder-width apart against a wall, your left knee bent, and your right leg straight and extended back (see figure 11.3).
2. Press your right heel to the floor.
3. Repeat with your left leg back.

Figure 11.3   Standing calf stretch.

Standing Hamstrings Stretch

1. Stand with your left leg forward and your right knee slightly bent.
2. Bend at the waist and reach with both arms toward your left toes while simultaneously bending your left toes toward your fingers (see figure 11.4).
3. Repeat with your other leg.

Figure 11.4   Standing hamstrings stretch.

Torso Stretch

1. Stand with your feet shoulder-width apart and your hands on your hips.
2. Slowly rotate your torso, in a circular motion, to the front, left, back, and right (see figure 11.5).
3. Repeat in the other direction.

Figure 11.5   Torso stretch.

Achilles Stretch

1. Stand with one leg slightly in front of the other.
2. Bend both knees slightly to stretch the calf (see figure 11.6).
3. Repeat with your other leg forward.

Figure 11.6 Achilles stretch.

Hip Adductor Stretch

1. Position yourself with your left knee bent and your left foot slightly toward the left; extend your right leg back while keeping your right foot parallel to your left foot. Extend your arms and place your hands even with your left foot (see figure 11.7).
2. Push forward with your left leg, but don't allow the knee to go over the toe.
3. Repeat with your right leg forward.

Figure 11.7 Hip adductor stretch.

Jump Rope Warm-Up Programs

The basic, intermediate, and advanced warm-up programs that follow should be performed at 60 to 80 percent of your MHR. To calculate your target heart rate, refer to chapter 5.

The basic 15 jumping techniques (level 1) are designed to simulate a wide range of athletic movements. Try to incorporate all of them into your total-body warm-up program. Rope jumping is an extremely effective training activity because you can use it to simulate and enhance a variety of athletic movements in 1 training session. The 15 basic jumping techniques—even when used in a warm-up—can help you develop balance, rhythm, timing, agility, coordination, quickness, speed, and power. The difference between jump rope warm-up programs and my high-intensity training programs is generally determined by intensity levels. The warm-up programs are generally associated with RPM levels of 160 and below, whereas the conditioning and training programs involve RPM of 180 and above. Warm-up programs should take 5 minutes or more.

BASIC WARM-UP PROGRAM

Use the shoulder measurement in the beginning. In order to correctly measure results, wait 1 week before you consider shortening the rope length.

TECHNIQUES

Bounce step, alternate-foot step, side straddle, forward straddle, skier's jump, bell jump

Training routine	1. Do 4 reps of the bounce step. 2. Do 4 reps of the alternate-foot step. 3. Repeat for 2.5 minutes. 4. Do 4 reps each of the side straddle, forward straddle, skier's jump, and bell jump. 5. Repeat for 2.5 minutes
Duration	5 minutes
Intensity	60-65% of MHR or 120-130 RPM
Goal	Move forward, backward, and laterally while jumping.

program

INTERMEDIATE WARM-UP PROGRAM

Use the shoulder measurement. In order to correctly measure results, wait 1 week before you consider adjusting the length of the rope.

TECHNIQUES

Bounce step, alternate-foot step, side straddle, forward straddle, skier's jump, bell jump, X-foot cross, full twister, arm crossover, power side swing jump

Training routine	1. Perform 8 reps of each technique. 2. Repeat for a total of 5 minutes.
Duration	5 minutes
Intensity	65-70% of MHR or 130-140 RPM
Goal	Move forward, backward, and laterally while jumping.

program

ADVANCED WARM-UP PROGRAM

Use the underarm measurement. Wait 1 week before you consider shortening the rope length.

TECHNIQUES

Bounce step, alternate-foot step, high step, side straddle, forward straddle, skier's jump, bell jump, full twister, X-foot cross, forward shuffle, backward shuffle, heel-to-toe, backward jumping, arm crossover, side swing jump, power jump

Training routine	1. Perform 12 reps of each technique. 2. Repeat for a total of 5 minutes.
Duration	5 minutes
Intensity	70-80% of MHR or 140-180 RPM
Goal	Move forward, backward, and laterally while jumping. Gradually increase intensity.

program

A Great Wrestling Warm-up for Developing Foot Speed and Coordination

As a competitive wrestler at the national and world levels, I believed in the power of the ropes for my daily training. Now a coach, I have used the Buddy Lee system with athletes at Central Michigan University, the University of Nebraska, the University of Missouri, and now Arizona State University. Rope jumping is a key part of our training. It provides an excellent tool for warm-up before wrestling; for developing hand and foot speed; for improving eye, hand, and foot coordination; and for increasing fitness. Our program at Arizona State has suffered over the years, and I am here to pick it back up and get these wrestlers jumping the correct way for championship wrestling. I believe the Buddy Lee jump rope training system will help us attain that winning edge.

Shawn Charles, world-class wrestler, head wrestling coach at Arizona State University

Injury Prevention and Rehabilitation

Injuries sometimes result from muscles and joints being undeveloped, overused, or unbalanced in strength and flexibility. In the case of injury—and after consulting your physician—you can use rope jumping to help you develop the balance, agility, and speed necessary to perform at high levels in your sport or in your quest to meet fitness goals. In either case, remember the old saying that "an ounce of prevention is worth a pound of cure." Train not only for performance but also for injury prevention. Listen to your body. Be aware of all indications of pending muscle strains and pulls. It is important to push your body during training and performance, but remember that it is better to slow down and take it easy when you sense that a muscle is tightening or you are experiencing an unusual level of fatigue. These are signals to stop and slow down. Ignoring them can result in a serious injury that means weeks or months of recovery.

Though rope jumping is an excellent training tool and can be used to help prevent and rehabilitate upper- and lower-body injuries, it is also important to be aware that injuries can occur during rope jumping itself. When rope jumping is performed incorrectly, it is no different from any other activity or sport in that there is always a risk of injury.

Rope Jumping as an Injury Prevention Strategy

Jump rope training can help you develop the motor skills necessary for high-level sports performance—the more motor skills you develop, the better you become and the better you perform in sports. Rope jumping can also go a long way toward strengthening your muscles, including the stabilizer muscles that support your ankles. Strengthened stabilizer muscles can reduce your risk of low and high ankle sprains. It makes more sense to learn how to prevent injuries than to spend time recovering from one. The costs of injury is far greater than the personal investment necessary to prevent many of them. Granted, you might not be able to predict all quirks of movement or situations that can result in serious injury. You can, however, minimize the effects of injury and the time required for recovery by recognizing that (so to speak) an ounce of prevention is worth more than a pound of treatment.

Rope jumping enhances your balance, agility, and speed, thus enabling you to make more efficient movements and reducing your risk of injury. One cause of injury is inadvertent loss of balance, and the importance of balance extends beyond sports performance. Balance, also known as equilibrium, is extremely important in everyday life. For example, we have all experienced losing our footing on a slippery floor or perhaps tripping on an object that lies unseen in our walking path. In such cases, a quick loss of balance can result in a fall or injury. What saves the day is our ability to quickly recover. Thus, exercises and training routines that develop balance can benefit you in everyday life.

Beyond daily life, numerous competitive sports severely test an athlete's sense of balance. These sports often require full-speed movements, changes of direction, and an ability to recover after being purposely knocked off balance—as in football, rugby, hockey, or lacrosse. In some other sports (e.g., gymnastics), performers are not purposely knocked off balance by other competitors but still face great demands for precision that test their ability to maintain balance and grace while executing complex movements. In these situations, poorly executed movements may result not only in lower scores but also in injury.

In addition to facilitating precise execution of complex sports movements, rope jumping offers a couple of built-in injury protection benefits. Rope jumping enhances proprioception in the feet and ankles in ways that reduce your risk of injury. Proprioceptive mechanisms are fascinating processes. It is proprioception, for example, that results in your recognition that your feet have landed properly or improperly during an athletic movement. This subtle awareness allows you to make slight adjustments in foot placement in future movements in ways that increase your precision and reduce your risk of injury. Highly developed proprioception can enable you to make precise foot placements in ways that increase your speed, quickness, and agility.

The colloquial phrase "ankle breakers" refers to the loss of balance and equilibrium experienced by a defensive player in, say, basketball or football when an offensive player executes a complex move. However, defensive players with high levels of proprioception, agility, and quickness are generally able to recover from the effects of feints and other offensive techniques. In either case, it is proprioception that allows athletes to execute or recover from feints and other complex and intricate athlete movements with minimal injury. Rope jumping—because of its reliance upon multiple major and minor muscle groups—increases proprioception, balance, and recovery of lost balance in ways that improve your agility, quickness, and balance while also reducing your risk of injury.

As with most athletic training programs, rope jumping requires that you proceed systematically and carefully in order to maximize training benefits while minimizing practice time. You can reduce your risk of injury by using proper attire and equipment and a good jumping surface. Mastering the basics and proper technique will lead you to noticeable training benefits while preparing you for sport-specific jump rope training programs.

Rope Jumping for Injury Rehabilitation

Rope jumping has always been a great tool for rehabilitation because it involves synchronizing and combining many movements for improved strength, conditioning, and flexibility. In sports, of course, injuries are eminent and usually result from muscle overuse or imbalance, poor technique, trauma, poor nutrition, fatigue, or lack of concentration.

Rope jumping has been used as a rehabilitation exercise for injured athletes searching for a progressive method to get back in shape while minimizing impact. As noted repeatedly in this book, rope jumping strengthens muscles that support the tendons and ligaments of the knees, feet, and ankles. Strengthening these supporting muscle groups reduces injury risk and contributes to recovery after injury. This strategy—strengthening muscles and muscle groups that support injured joints, tendons, or ligaments—is practiced in most rehabilitation programs.

When rehabilitating injury in the ankles, feet, or knees, first try a lower-impact activity such as the stationary bike, swimming, or jogging in order to build some strength. Then switch to rope jumping as a graded exercise for improving proprioception and strength in the feet, ankles, knees, wrists, and shoulders. Aim for low impact, low height, and short contact with the jumping surface. Be light on the balls of your feet.

In addition to minimizing ankle injuries, rope jumping also strengthens the calves, quadriceps, hamstrings, and glutes. In addition to contributing to speed and explosiveness, these muscles also support ligaments and tendons that stabilize the entire knee structure, including the patellar tendon As with other physical activities, rope jumping is not recommended while you are undergoing the early stages of an injury healing process. However, once the knee joint is strong enough to comfortably manage your body weight, you can incorporate low levels of jump rope training (ideally on a high-rebounding surface) to enhance the rehabilitation process.

Initially, a delicate and low-intensity (100–120 RPM) bounce step is the best rope jumping technique for rehabilitation. I recommend doing 3 of these sessions per week and slowly increasing intensity and duration levels every 4 weeks to allow the knee joint to stabilize while the supporting muscle groups are strengthened. It is important to consult your physician or other health care practitioner before incorporating rope jumping into your rehab program. Once you have done this, remember my cardinal rule of jumping: Jump no more than an inch (2.5 cm) from the surface and land gracefully on the balls of your feet. This technique allows your calves, quadriceps, and hamstrings to absorb the impact of each jump.

Rope jumping can also help athletes improve gripping strength and strengthen muscle groups (including stabilizer muscles) that support the hands, wrists, and elbows—especially important for athletes who play racquet sports or sports requiring throwing or tossing motions (e.g., tennis). These benefits are generated through the effects of the literally hundreds of repetitive wrist turns executed during each rope jumping session. These turns of the wrist draw upon muscle groups responsible for fine motor skills—those actions required for finger, hand, and wrist movements as well as eye-hand coordination, which carry over to catching, throwing, or tossing movements. In addition to developing eye–hand coordination, these movements develop fast-twitch muscle fibers in the forearms, deltoids, and shoulders.

Thus rope jumping can benefit muscle groups and muscle fibers required for execution in nearly every sport and every athletic or training movement. Rope jumping is not only an ideal training technique but also one that can prevent injury. If you jump rope according to my cardinal rule, you will strengthen muscle groups that support your feet, ankles, and knees—and therefore reduce your risk of injury.

Rehabilitation Programs

Following are a number of programs for injury rehabilitation. Each program is designed for use during rehabilitation of specific injuries.

ANKLE REHABILITATION PROGRAM

Jump rope increases kinesthetic awareness and proprioception in the ankles. The impact is minimal if, according to my cardinal rule of jumping, you are jumping less than 3/4 inch (1.9 cm) off the floor.

ROPE MEASUREMENT

Use the shoulder measurement.

TECHNIQUES

Basic bounce step, the alternate-foot step, and the single-leg jump with timing and control.

Training routine	1. Jump for 30 seconds using the basic bounce, then rest for 1 minute. 2. Jump for 30 seconds (first on one leg for 4 counts, then on the other leg for 4 counts), then rest for 1 minute. 3. Jump for 30 seconds using the alternate-foot step, then rest for 1 min. 4. Jump for 30 seconds using a combination of the basic bounce and the alternate-foot step, then rest for 1 minute. 5. Jump for 30 seconds (first on one leg for 4 counts, then on the other leg for 4 counts), then rest for 1 minute. 6. Repeat the sequence.
Duration	5 minutes (10 sets of 30 seconds each)
Goal	Maintain good form while minimizing impact.

program

HAND AND WRIST REHABILITATION PROGRAM

Rope jumping is an ideal exercise for rehabilitating the hands and wrists because of the forces involved in executing circular motion to turn the rope. As a result, jumping rope improves the gripping dynamics of the hand, and the fast-turning wrist motion involved in rope jumping is highly beneficial for athletes who are rehabilitating a hand or wrist.

ROPE MEASUREMENT

Use the underarm measurement.

TECHNIQUE

Alternate footstep.

Training routine	1. Sprint with the alternate-foot step for 20 seconds, then rest for 1 minute. 2. Repeat 5 times.
Duration	2 minutes (4 sets at 30 seconds each)
Goal	Maintain good form. Concentrate on a firm and light grip.

program

SHOULDER REHABILITATION PROGRAM

Rope jumping develops muscular endurance in the shoulders because the movements required strengthen the anterior and posterior shoulder muscles, including the deltoid and infraspinatus.

ROPE MEASUREMENT

Use the underarm measurement.

TECHNIQUES

Arm crossover, side swing jump, alternate-foot step, basic bounce step.

Training routine	1. Jump backward for 1 minute, then rest for 1 minute.
	2. Jump with the arm crossover for 1 minute, then rest for 1 minute.
	3. Jump backward and forward for 1 minute, then rest for 1 minute.
	4. Jump with the side swing jump for 1 minute, then rest for 1 minute.
	5. Jump backward with the alternate-foot step for 1 minute, then rest for 1 minute.
Duration	5 minutes (includes jumping backward)
Goal	Maintain good form. Concentrate on small circles with the wrists.

program

KNEE REHABILITATION PROGRAM

Rope jumping can be used to rehabilitate injured knees because the up-and-down motion of rope jumping strengthens the ligaments surrounded by the articular cartilage and meniscus of the knee. Once the knee joint is strong enough to comfortably manage your body weight, you can incorporate low levels of jump rope training (ideally on a high-rebounding surface) to enhance the rehabilitation process.

ROPE MEASUREMENT

Use the shoulder measurement.

TECHNIQUES

Basic bounce, alternate-foot step, side straddle, forward straddle, skier's jump, bell jump, X-foot cross.

Training routine	1. 4 basic bounce, 4 alternate-foot step (counting right foot only). Repeat for a total of 1 minute, then rest for 1 minute. 2. 4 side straddle, 4 forward straddle. Repeat for a total of 1 minute, then rest for 1 minute. 3. 4 skier's jump, 4 bell jumps. Repeat for a total of 1 minute, then rest for 1 minute. 4. 4 side straddle, 4 X-foot cross. Repeat for a total of 1 minute, then rest for 1 minute. 5. 4 basic bounce, 4 alternate-foot step. Repeat for a total of 1 minute, then rest for 1 minute.
Duration	5 minutes (5 sets of 1 minute each)
Goal	Maintain good form while minimizing impact.

program

CHAPTER

13

Weight Loss for Athletic Goals

Your sport's off-season is probably the best time to drop those extra pounds accumulated during the postseason. That's because the post-season is typically a time when athletes rest and recover from the physical and psychological grind of in-season competition. The post-season is normally allocated to healing from injuries, recovering physical strength, and for those athletes who have had an injury-free competitive season, the post season is an opportunity to get an early start on improving technique or beginning new training programs. Maintaining a high level of physical fitness during this critical time period is crucial to staying on top of your sport—or making the team next season. Ideally, you should enter the preseason not only at a high level of fitness but also at a body weight that allows you improve sport-specific movements that will lead to high performance during preseason training and practice sessions. However, some athletes may put on extra weight during the post-season because they have not modified their dietary or nutritional practices to account for their reduced physical activity. Many of these athletes may need a post-season training or workout program that helps maintain or increase fitness without making excessive demands upon time required for healing and recovery.

Jump rope training is an ideal off-season training technique for improving fitness, sports performance, and burning calories without a large investment of time. As a multijoint movement that incorporates all muscle groups, it ranks as one of the most efficient ways to burn calories and control weight gain that can take place in the post-season. More importantly, when performed in short training sessions at high intensity levels, rope jumping can burn excess calories while you are healing from the physical demands of your sport. High-intensity workouts performed at 80-95 percent of your maximum heart rate (MHR) can burn up to 14 calories per minute and boost your fat-burning metabolism for up to 24 hours after the exercise session. Aerobic exercise sessions burn high levels of fat during exercise but low levels of fat after the exercise session. Anaerobic exercise burns low levels of fat during the exercise session but high levels of fat 24-48 hours after the exercise session. Therefore anaerobic intensity levels are an ideal strategy to control weight gain without requiring long periods of training time.

For example, according to the American College of Sports Medicine (ACSM), the combination of frequency, intensity, and duration have been found to produce a training effect. A training effect can be defined as an elevation of metabolism produced by exercise. For example, metabolic increases in the burning of calories and anabolic effects that lead to building muscle are training goals of most athletes. ACSM reports that these effects can be determined by levels of physical stimulus, i.e., exercise intensity levels. The lower the level of intensity, the lower the training effects. The greater the intensity level, the greater the training effects. Training at low levels of intensity will require longer periods of time to generate training effects. Training at high levels of intensity therefore can create noticeable training effects in short periods of time. Rather than jumping rope at low intensity levels, my high-intensity jump rope training system increases your metabolism and pushes your heart rate up to at least 80 percent of its maximum so that you can improve fitness and control your weight while recovering from the demands of your sports competitions. Maintenance of fitness and proper weight can translate directly in better sports performance when your season begins.

Jumping Rope for Weight Loss

Weight loss routines are a highly sought-after commodity these days. In addition to the cosmetics of weight loss (e.g., making people feel as if their clothes fit properly), there is growing evidence that it offers significant health benefits. This is especially true for individuals who have a high body mass index or high levels of body fat. This is especially important for athletes. Extra weight increases stress on the joints, muscles and cardiovascular system which cannot only reduce performance, but increases risk of injury.

Athletes, however, are exposed to the same dietary risks as non-athletes. The convenience of fast-food and carbohydrate-rich snacks that can be loaded with chemicals, preservatives, hormones and other ingredients can have negative effects on health. These effects may be especially risky for athletes during the post-season, when they are less likely to burn off these extra calories at levels that take place during the in-season. Relaxation and recovery can also include temptations to relax dietary discipline, which can result in extra weight while also detracting from fitness levels. Therefore, the combination of relaxed dietary practices and reduced physical activity can have relatively similar effects on even the best conditioned athletes as less-fit individuals. These results include increases in cholesterol levels, triglycerides, and, in some cases, insulin resistance.

Therefore, athletes must not become influenced by temptations to believe that weight loss can result from one process, one activity, one pill, or one exercise. Two principles are emerging as critical components of any weight loss strategy. First, increase your basal metabolic rate (BMR)—the rate at which your body burns energy when you are completely at rest. Second, build lean muscle mass, which is important because it leads to an increase in metabolism and the burning of body fat. An intelligent diet, even in the post-season, can help you maintain proper body weight. More importantly, by increasing your knowledge of nutrition, you can still enjoy eating a reasonable quantity of tasty food without incurring health risks.

Do More Than One Thing at a Time

Fitness experts agree that people can effectively manage weight by making changes in what they eat, how much they eat, and when and how often they eat. Most experts recommend consuming several small meals per day rather than three large ones. These include the following:

1. Protein-rich breakfast
2. Midmorning snack
3. Protein-packed nutritious lunch
4. Midafternoon snack
5. Protein- and vegetable-rich dinner

Some athletes and fitness enthusiasts consume up to eight meals and snacks per day. Most competitive athletes eat five to six meals and snacks per day. This may seem like a lot of food, but research has found that consuming multiple small meals and nutritious snacks each day boosts metabolism. Ideally, you should eat every two hours, the approximate feeding cycle of infants! These multiple meals also help your body maintain healthy levels of blood sugar, thus helping to prevent cravings. Cravings can lead to consumption of high levels of high-glycemic and high-fat foods that cause undesired weight gain. Because of the significance of muscle mass in metabolism—and the fact that increased metabolism regulates weight—most experts suggest that people consume sufficient levels of protein per pound of body weight. Protein requirements can be determined by the demands of your sport. Some bodybuilders, for example, attempt to consume 1 gram of protein for each pound of body weight. Ideally, most athletes should strive for at least a half gram of protein for each pound of body weight. These portions reduce the prospects of catabolism, the breakdown of protein for energy, which can negatively impact performance, immune system function, and psychological well-being. You should also reduce your carbohydrate consumption to about 30 percent of your diet and your fat consumption to an even lower percentage. In addition, it is recommended that you consume 20 to 30 grams of fiber per day. Fiber consumption reduces cravings, protects against high cholesterol, and contributes to the overall health of your digestion and elimination system.

Suggestions for Food Intake and Losing Weight for Athletes

- Eat 5 to 8 small meals a day, including fruit snacks (e.g., bananas, which are a great source of potassium).
- Drink water; avoid sodas and alcoholic drinks.
- Avoid eating sweets; replace sugar with organic honey, maple syrup, agave nectar, or stevia extract.
- Keep fat intake low; avoid butter, margarine, cream, and oil in cooking and on meat, as well as in fried foods. Use olive oil to cook. Avoid eating fast food.
- Bake or steam food; do not fry.
- Stay away from breads made with white flour (e.g., hot dog and hamburger buns). Eat whole-grain breads instead.
- Eat well-balanced meals every day that include fruits, vegetables, fish (choose fish that contain less mercury), and white meats.
- Vary the foods you consume.
- Eat foods rich in antioxidants (e.g., leafy vegetables, berries, garlic, turmeric).
- Juice veggies and fruits at least twice a week.
- Consume protein in white meat, fish, poultry, tofu, and nuts. Eat eggs in moderation; their yolk is very high in cholesterol.
- Get 8 hours of sleep and, when possible, a midday power nap of 30 to 60 minutes.
- Try to eat your biggest meal during the day and your last meal or snack 4 hours before going to bed—before 6 p.m.
- Jump rope 3 to 5 times a week at a higher intensity for weight loss.

Stay Hydrated

Your body is about 70 percent water, which is critical for proper metabolism, brain function, and sports performance. Water also helps eliminate fatigue, reduced coordination, and muscle cramping. It is important to replace lost fluids as your exercise intensity increases. A loss of 2 percent of body weight in fluid has been linked to a drop in blood volume for elite athletes. This condition causes the heart to work harder in order to move blood through the bloodstream to the working muscles. The International Marathon Medical Directors Association recommends drinking a sports drink that contains sodium, potassium, and essential electrolytes when you exercise for 30 minutes or more.

At the same time, remember that there can be too much of a good thing. Though drinking enough water is critical to athletic performance, you must manage hydration properly in order to prevent hyponatremia or "water intoxication." Drinking too much water during periods of exertion can flush your body of sodium, leading the sodium-starved brain to swell against the skull to the point of causing nausea, weakness, seizures, and, in extreme cases, coma and death. A good rule that I follow is to drink when I become thirsty; this may seem obvious, but in the rush of daily life we do not always practice it.

Another way to determine hydration levels is to become aware of the color of your urine. If your urine is clear, then you are sufficiently hydrated. Dark colored urine can be a sign of dehydration. Also, because of the close proximity in the brain of hunger and thirst centers, it is possible that you may actually require fluids when you may "feel" hungry. This is why many people have reported a reduction in hunger and cravings after drinking fluids. Therefore, increasing fluid intake can also reduce unnecessary food consumption and further help regulate bodyweight.

Watch Sodium Intake

Salt or sodium is an essential nutrient in the human diet, and especially so for athletes, because it helps regulate fluid balance and supports proper muscle function. Sodium needs vary from person to person, but the healthy dose is about 1 teaspoon of salt per day. Athletes need more sodium because on days of heavy training they lose sodium through sweat. The recommended amount of sodium during exercise depends on how much sweat is being produced. When doing heavy training for 3 hours, for example, your total sweat loss includes 3,375 milligrams of sodium. As an athlete, then, you should be aware of the sodium you lose during heavy sweating and consume a sports drink or salty food to replace your lost sodium. If you are involved in triathlons or ultramarathons, be sure to consume 100 to 250 milligrams of sodium for every 8 ounces of water you drink.

As with water, excessive sodium consumption can lead to problems—in this case, high blood pressure, which in turn can lead to hypertension. It can also lead to water retention, which is a major cause of weight gain. You are at greater risk for these problems if you eat a lot of fast food or packaged "convenience" foods (even drinks such as soda and concentrate-based fruit juice can be high in both sugar and salt). If your body retains excessive water, you will carry around extra weight.

Exercise

A number of medical authorities have reported that if there is a fountain of youth, it is regular exercise. Discussion of how much exercise is necessary to manage weight, however, has changed dramatically over the past 30 years. Initially, scientific research reported that exercising for 20 minutes three times a week at 70 percent of your maximum heart rate was enough to result in a measurable training effect (determined by increases in overall endurance and stamina). Today, fitness enthusiasts and sports performers want more than barely measurable increases. People want fitness and performance gains that result in feeling and looking not just better but great. These individuals need higher intensities and frequencies of fitness training.

Medical authorities have joined the fitness bandwagon and now recommend that individuals incorporate 30 minutes or more of cardio at least 5 days a week to reduce undesired weight levels. They recommend that this cardio activity be conducted at 70 percent of MHR or higher. This frequency and intensity not only helps you manage diet and hydration but can also result in significant reductions in body fat and excess weight in weeks rather than months. These strategies have been incorporated into several popular television shows about fitness. As much as people would prefer quick and easy strategies for weight loss, combining diet and exercise seems to be the best formula.

Train Anaerobically

Research-based approaches to weight loss have also incorporated another strategy into weight management programs: resistance and anaerobic training. Weight loss experts have realized that anaerobic training and exercise boosts metabolism and promotes the burning of body fat for longer periods than does aerobic training. Many fitness experts suggest that the fat-burning benefit of 20 to 30 minutes of anaerobic training—particularly, high-intensity interval training (HIIT)—exceeds that of

1 hour (or more) of aerobic exercise. This training and fitness option may work particularly well for people who juggle multiple responsibilities and thus have to find ways to squeeze fitness and training into a busy schedule.

Resistance training is now a popular weight-loss strategy because the more muscle you build the more fat you burn. Some people may become discouraged by recognizing that resistance training can result in initial *increases* in weight, but they should be patient. This increase may actually be added muscle. People should continue with their resistance training, cardio workouts, and dietary discipline until the fat starts "melting away."

Jump Rope Programs for Weight Loss

Rope jumping can be easily incorporated into your weight loss or weight regulation routine. You can use my programs to add high-intensity interval training that helps your body burn fat for several hours or days after a workout. My programs specifically target the anaerobic energy system and can boost your workout intensity to 85 to 95 percent of your MHR. Although these intensity levels draw upon glucose and glycogen, your body will become conditioned to break down fat into sugar (glucose and glycogen) to replenish these energy stores.

You can tailor your rope jumping program to serve as an effective anaerobic training program in conjunction with resistance training or cardio activity. Because rope jumping is a portable exercise, you can use it as an anaerobic training routine at your office or home. You won't even need to go to a gym. You can use the alternate-foot step, the bounce step, and other jumping techniques in combination at an intensity level of at least 140 RPM. You can break your sessions into sets of 120 to 240 jumps at a time. By the time you take short breaks (15 to 30 seconds between sets), you should have jumped rope for up to 30 minutes, excluding breaks, in your session. This is an ideal time period for most cardio routines because it provides enough time for your body to raise metabolism to training levels and maintain those levels long enough to produce a training effect. You can also mix an anaerobic component into this routine by integrating several high-intensity bouts of jumping and therefore reap the weight loss benefits of aerobic and anaerobic exercise. Aerobic intensity levels should exceed 180 RPM.

WEIGHT LOSS PROGRAM LEVEL 1

Off-season and preseason

Use the shoulder measurement in the beginning. In order to correctly measure results, wait 1 week before you consider shortening the rope length.

3 to 5 times per week.

All 15 basic techniques.

Training routine	1. Jump rope for 2 minutes (incorporate all 15 basic techniques). 2. Do light calisthenics (push-ups, sit-ups, dips) for 1 minute. 3. Repeat 10 times.
Duration	30 minutes
Intensity	140 to 160 RPM = 70-75% of the MHR
Goal	Focus on performing good technique with smooth transition.

program

WEIGHT LOSS PROGRAM LEVEL 2

SEASON

Off-season and preseason

ROPE MEASUREMENT

Use the shoulder measurement in the beginning. In order to correctly measure results, wait 1 week before you consider shortening the rope length.

FREQUENCY

3 to 5 times per week

TECHNIQUES

Alternate-foot step and high step

Training routine	1. Jump rope for 5 minutes (alternate-foot step and high step) using all planes (forward, backward, lateral). During the last 10 seconds of every minute, do a sprint (alternate-foot step) at 85 to 95 percent of MHR. 2. Do light calisthenics (pull-ups, sit-ups, lunges) for 1 minute. 3. Repeat 5 times.
Duration	30 minutes
Intensity	160 to 180 RPM = 75-80% of the MHR. Sprints at 220+ RPM = 90% of the MHR
Goal	Being able to move from 10-second sprints to calisthenics with little to no rest time.

program

WEIGHT LOSS PROGRAM LEVEL 3

SEASON

Off-season and preseason

ROPE MEASUREMENT

Use the shoulder measurement in the beginning. In order to correctly measure results, wait 1 week before you consider shortening the rope length.

FREQUENCY

3 to 5 times per week

TECHNIQUES

All 15 basic techniques

Training routine	1. Jump rope for 9 minutes (incorporating all 15 basic techniques). During the last 10 seconds of every minute, do a sprint (alternate-foot step) at 85 to 95 percent of MHR. 2. Do light calisthenics (pull-ups, sit-ups, lunges) for 1 minute. 3. Repeat 3 times.
Duration	30 minutes
Intensity	180 to 220 RPM = 80-90% of the MHR
Goal	Being able to move from 10-second sprints to calisthenics with no rest time.

program

About the Author

Buddy Lee is known as one of the world's top experts in jump rope conditioning. He has earned a worldwide reputation with his incredible jump rope skills, putting on 6,000 shows in 50 countries and appearing in TV commercials and talk shows. He has also appeared on CNN Headline News and in *Business Week* and *Parade* magazines.

Lee is the president and CEO of Jump Rope Tech Technology, Inc., the leading expert in the field of jump rope training for improved sport performance. He is the founder of the Jump Rope Institute and co-inventor and patent holder of Buddy Lee Speed Ropes, the ropes used by U.S. Olympic athletes.

A retired US Marine and U.S. Olympian in wrestling, Buddy now consults with strength and conditioning coaches worldwide as well as elite athletes from various disciplines. Many fitness organizations, such as CrossFit, TRX, KettleBell, HopSports, and MMA, have integrated Buddy Lee's program into their systems. He lives in northern Virginia.

To learn more about Buddy Lee and his training programs, visit www.buddyleejumpropes.com.